Nancy Lieberman. Lou Vairo. Bruce Baumgartner. Mark Gubicza. Phil McConkey. Jackie Joyner-Kersee. Mike Richter. Seven world-class athletes, coaches, and leaders.

In the pages of Crunch Time, they share with you their experiences at the top of amateur and professional sports, their highs and lows, and the very real personal challenges they've faced. Seven fascinating personalities offer their insights on managing crisis in sports, and more importantly, in life.

Crunch Time

7 sports legends on managing crisis

Brian P. Dunleavy

A Strawberry Book
www.strawberrybooks.com

SB

Strawberry Books is a publishing house that thrills, delights and informs our
readers with high-quality e-books, physical books and online content.

Please check out our website and follow us on Twitter:

@thrillsdelights

For Eileen, with love

Table of Contents

Introduction

Crunch Time.

You've been there.

It's when the clock is winding down and the game, or your job, is on the line. It's when you're trying to keep your head, while all about you people are losing theirs, and blaming it on you.

It's when you are being criticized in a public way, perhaps for something you did not even do. It's when miscommunication leads to conflict, and you need to resolve that conflict, quickly and in a way everyone can live with.

In a grimmer vein, it's when a loved one is sick, maybe even gravely ill, and is depending on you to help them.

Crunch Time is when crisis comes.

Great athletes and coaches face Crunch Time on a regular basis. Their successes and failures, victories and defeats, adulation and humiliation, take place on a grand stage. We watch them win, and we watch them lose. We see them rise to great heights, and we witness their fall.

Each of the sports figures in this book has faced Crunch Time again and again, both on the field, and often, in their personal and work lives. All of them, in their own way, are amazing people. Gifted, yes, but more than gifted.

To reach the pinnacle of a sport—any sport—takes more than natural talent. It also takes hard work, confidence, courage, commitment and smarts. All of us in the "real" world can use a little inspiration to see us through the difficult times, and great sports figures are as good a source of inspiration as any. However, losing a game—any game—isn't the same thing as losing a loved one, or having your reputation damaged, or experiencing failure in business. And Knute Rockne-esque speeches don't generally spark long-term motivation and commitment.

I have read many of the books written by athletes and coaches that have graced the best-seller lists in recent years. What I set out to do with this book was to take some of the best aspects of those other books – glimpses inside the minds of people at the top of their games - while offering something different: real-world lessons that you can use, both in the business world, and in life.

As a lifelong sports fan, I have witnessed some breathtaking moments. I celebrated with the nation during the run of the 1980 "Miracle on Ice" gold medal-winning US Olympic hockey team; I was endlessly entertained by the "Bronx Zoo" New York Yankees World Series teams of the late 1970s, and the Bronx Bombers' return to glory under Joe Torre in the late 1990s and early 2000s.

I admired the toughness of Bill Parcells' New York Giants Super Bowl championship teams in 1986 and 1991; and breathed a huge sigh of relief when the New York Rangers finally ended "the curse" after 54 years and won the Stanley Cup in 1994. As a professional sports reporter, I had the pleasure of covering the Giants' surprising run to the Super Bowl in 2001.

Although many books have come out of each of these journeys to glory, none of them have been focused specifically on the crises each of these great teams faced—and overcame. Indeed, until now, most books written by sports legends have been heavy on platitudes and clichés, and light on guidance.

However, the sports leaders interviewed herein—Bruce Baumgartner, Mark Gubicza, Jackie Joyner-Kersee, Nancy Lieberman, Phil McConkey, Mike Richter and Lou Vairo—were selected not only because they have been successful and well known in their respective sports—but because they have faced unique crises themselves, either in their professional or personal lives, or both.

These folks also have experience that transcends the sports world. Many of them are involved in their own business ventures, or serve in executive positions within their respective sports, meaning that they are not merely attempting to translate lessons from the field into business, but they are actively involved in applying them.

Each of the following chapters is presented in an easy-to-read Q&A format that focuses the discussion on crises faced and specific lessons learned. Also, at the conclusion of each chapter, there is a "Key Messages" section that summarizes the important, actionable points discussed.

I hope you agree that *Crunch Time* offers unique perspectives on dealing with times of crisis, and does so in an enlightening and entertaining fashion.

The clock is ticking: when crisis comes, will you be ready?

Chapter One

Nancy Lieberman: Basketball Pioneer

Nancy Lieberman challenges herself as much if not more than any other top sports figure in the modern era. Known as "Lady Magic," she joined USA Basketball women's national team for the 1975 Pan American Games at 17 (she was three years younger than the next youngest player on the team), helping the team to an undefeated record and a gold medal in the tournament while competing against players older and more experienced.

She stayed with the team for the 1976 Summer Olympics in Montreal, the first-ever Olympic tournament for women's basketball, and keyed its run to a silver medal. At the time, at age 18, she was the youngest American basketball player to win a medal in international competition.

After the Olympics, the Brooklyn-born Lieberman enrolled at Old Dominion University in Norfolk, Virginia, where she starred for the school's women's basketball team, leading it to two national championships and a Women's National Invitational Tournament title in four years. She still holds the school record for assists (961) and scored more than 2,400 points and grabbed more than 1,100 rebounds during her time at ODU. She twice won the Wade Award as the best collegiate women's player in the country, and again led the US national team to a silver medal during the 1979 Pan American Games in Puerto Rico.

Lieberman's success as a female athlete in the 1970s meant that her fame soon expanded beyond the relatively friendly confines of the basketball world. As issues surrounding gender politics and the sexual revolution were the subject of heated debates in the public discourse—and women marched on Washington, DC in support of the Equal Rights Amendment—athletes such as Lieberman, fellow basketball star Ann Meyers and tennis legend Billie Jean King became standard bearers for these causes—and not always by design. King may have been an established—and stalwart—activist, but Meyers and Lieberman were still in college. Lieberman just wanted to continue playing the game she loved.

At the time, there weren't many options for women basketball players who wanted professional careers in the sport. After leaving ODU in 1980, Lieberman bounced around between the Women's Professional Basketball League, which folded in 1982, and the United States Basketball League (USBL), a minor men's league several rungs below the National Basketball Association (NBA).

She also had a stint with the Washington Generals, the team that has played patsies to the Harlem Globetrotters for decades. She hung around long enough to play for the Phoenix Mercury of the Women's National Basketball Association (WNBA) during the league's inaugural season in 1997. By then, she was 39 and her best days as a player were behind her.

For Lieberman, it was on to the next challenge: In 1998, she was hired as the coach and general manager of the WNBA's Detroit Shock, but left the team after three years amid allegations (made by unnamed players) that she had a sexual affair with one of the team's players. She denies the allegations to this day, but was still left in the position of resurrecting her career—again—and she has done so successfully.

After several years of working as a women's basketball analyst with ESPN, she was hired in 2009 as the head coach of the Texas Legends of the NBA Development League, making her the first woman to coach a US men's professional team. In another first, she became the team's assistant general manager.

She is still blazing new trails: In August 2015, she was hired as an assistant coach by the NBA's Sacramento Kings. She is the second woman to serve as a coach with an NBA team (Becky Hammon currently works with the San Antonio Spurs).

Crunch Time caught up with Lieberman at her home in Dallas before the start of NBA training camp.

Crunch Time: Women who are playing professional team sports today really owe a debt of gratitude to athletes such as you, Ann Meyers and Billie Jean King and what you were able to achieve in the 1970s and 1980s. Were you aware of what you were doing to change the perception of women's sports or were you just going out there and playing ball and playing the game that you loved to play?

Nancy Lieberman: Well I think we would all be not telling the truth if we said we started to play sports to be game changers. Nobody has that crystal ball. We played because it was fun, we played because it was competitive and we played because we loved what we did and that was really important to us, whether you're talking about Billie [Jean King] or Ann [Meyers] or myself.

That said, after awhile, I understood at a certain point that I was a gatekeeper to women's sports. When you're young and you're in the now and you're kind of electric and you're winning championships, you're that player, you know that there's a little bit more inherent responsibility than just playing basketball. And I knew that by my freshman year in college.

In the locker room during the 1976 Olympics, we were sitting there getting ready for the silver medal game. As a young player, I am just happy to be there, but our coach, Billie Jean Moore, comes in and says, "What we do today, ladies, when we win, this will change women's basketball and women's sports for the next 25 years."

You think, what does that mean? But now I get it. I mean, I see the benefits of what happened in 1976 with that Olympic team and that silver medal. And that was the first time women's basketball was ever in Olympic sports. So years later I could understand the magnitude of that; I just didn't see it when I was living it.

CT: Then you get to ODU, and you become the face of the program, at 18. That's a heavy responsibility at a young age.

NL: Yeah, suddenly I was at Rotary Clubs, I was at Kiwanis Clubs. I'm like, "I thought I came here to play basketball!"

I was straight from New York and they said, "You have to do this. You have to grow the game. You have to understand you're an ambassador of the game." I said, "What do you mean I'm the ambassador of the game? I'm a kid!"

But there was a huge awareness of what players like Ann and I were doing. And we had to live up to that.

CT: How did you manage that at such a young age?

NL: It is a little daunting because I just wanted to play to win, and all the other residual stuff was hard to grasp at that point. It is overwhelming, but I had a friend, [sportscaster] Dick Schaap. He just kind of put his little wing over me and he was so instrumental, like if I wasn't sure about something, I would call Dick and say, "Hey, they want me to do this or do I have to go on 'Good Morning America' with Jane Pauley? Or the 'Today Show?'" And he would tell me I had to do it and walk me through what to say and how to handle myself.

He reminded me to be mindful of what I was saying because I was not only representing myself but my generation of women's basketball players and athletes. He would say, "Nancy, whatever you say is going to have validity and credibility with men." I'll never forget Dick saying this to me my sophomore year; he said, "When [women's sports] get on the big board at Vegas, when you start having recruiting violations and men start watching you, you've made it." And what he was saying is that people like Ann and I were going to make people care about women's basketball. And so my job became to make people care.

CT: Having a mentor like Dick Schaap, a fellow New Yorker and legendary sports journalist, must have been incredibly

important for you at that young age. How did you meet him and how did he kind of develop into that role for you?

NL: Dick came down to Norfolk to do a story on me my freshman year and his warmth and kindness and his approach to people was magnetic. He said, "You know, if you ever need anything, I will help you, and then he started inviting me to play tennis with him up in New York.

I can remember going to the tennis club with him and we'd go have lunch with [Dick's wife] Trish and I would have [their son and now sportscaster] Jeremy on my lap. How about that? I'd be bouncing little Jeremy on my knee...

Dick was always there for me. He never forced anything on me but he said, "Nancy, life's about selecting friends and being kind." He introduced me to Muhammad Ali... Imagine that as a young kid?

But Dick just always gave me a little bit of reason because when you're young, you're living day to day, you're in the now. When you get a little older, you get perspective, that it's not about you, it's about the people around you and how you live and treat others.

CT: I had a friend who went to Old Dominion around the same time you did and he always talks about the culture in Norfolk. Do you think that there was something about the city and the surrounding area there that made your team particularly attractive to them and engaging to them?

NL: My athletic director, Dr. [Jim] Jarrett, was a visionary. There wasn't a day that went by that a Lady Monarch wasn't in the community. So on our worst days, when we lost one or two in a row my freshman year, because we were out in the community so much, they didn't boo us, they treated us like family members. They just never left our side. And that's phenomenal. But that was because we became part of their family, not just athletes. It was really kind of cool.

CT: You know, I think given the fact that you're at a young age and going through all of this stuff and being seen as an ambassador for the sport, I'm imagining that having a mentor like Dick and having that kind of a supportive network of community around you probably helped you through that process. Would you say it was key?

NL: Oh absolutely because I didn't have my dad [Author's note: Nancy parents divorced when she was a child.], I really didn't have a lot of parental support. I didn't really have that mentor in my life or that family member that I could go to and say, "Hey, I'm scared or I'm not sure… What do I do?"

In many cases, Dick was that person to me probably more than he knew. He and his wife treated me like I was their other kid. I remember him taking me to a celebrity tennis tournament in Las Vegas right after my senior year, and I'm sitting there at a banquet and they bring you the sorbet after your salad, and I'm like, "This is it? That's all I get?" [She laughs.] Dick was just sitting next to me I'm sure laughing his pants off because I didn't know what fork to use, what glass to drink from.

But Dick was preparing me for what was in front of me. He knew that I would be a focal point of women's athletics for a long time and here's this guy, never made me feel bad but he understood the magnitude of my position before I understood the magnitude of my position. And Dick very gently guided me. Everywhere I went, he'd ask, "What are you going to wear?" He'd tell me, "When you sign autographs, don't look at your autograph, look at the person." He told me how to talk to people, how to accept and return compliments. Just little tips. He said, "Any time you get an award, you should love it like it's the first award you've ever received." He told me that when I spoke to a reporter I should ask after their family, things like that. Little things, but they prepared me for where I was about to go in my career.

CT: So now you've reached the pinnacle of college athletics. You've represented the US on the international level. Were you frustrated at that point that there still wasn't the infrastructure for you to carry on your career as a professional here in the US and play and continue that level of notoriety and continue the growth of women's sports?

NL: So leaving college, I just had this mentality that I'd go through college, we'd win championships and I'd get drafted in the first women's league, the WBL, as the number one pick. Things were kind of on course for me in a very unrealistic way.

The Dallas Diamonds paid me $100,000 in 1980. I moved to Dallas. I'm playing professional basketball, and we get all the way to the fifth game of the championship against Nebraska. We lost, but things were kind of going the way I thought they should for me at 22 years old.

But when the WBL folded is when I was like, "Oh, my gosh, what am I going to do? I was so used to being Nancy Lieberman and coddled and people kissing my behind and telling me how great I was… I didn't know me. I can look back today and say I didn't have high self-esteem. I was scared. I didn't really know who I was because I never really had to engage that person. It was more the adulation of the fans. I couldn't express that to you thirty-five years ago, but I realize that back then I was like, "Oh my God, is anybody going to like me?"

There's no women's league, there's nothing. From 1974 until 1981, all I had known was Team USA, winning medals, representing America, standing on podiums, championships at Old Dominion, signing autographs, getting thousands of letters from people telling me that I inspired them, that I changed their lives… Then it was gone in an instant. I was scared to death. I was like, "What am I going to do?"

Eventually I signed to play in the USBL.

CT: During this time you also worked with tennis legend Martina Navratilova… She credited you with helping her career.

NL: We were at the US Open in, I think 1983, and a guy came up to me and said, "Are you Martina's coach?" I went nuts. I wanted to tell the guy, "Hey, I'm a basketball player! One of the best in the world." But it was frustrating. I wasn't playing. I was just training with Martina five hours a day. At least she got to go out on the court. I had nowhere to play. Until the USBL came along.

There are so many moments in one's life where you turn around and go, "How did this happen? Why did that happen?" That time was good for me because I had to learn a little humility. There were just certain things that I had to learn about myself, but I was also helping somebody and learning from them, too.

CT: During that time you were practicing with the Los Angeles Lakers under Pat Riley. Between that and your time in the USBL, that must have helped set the stage for what you're doing now. I mean, you don't need to prove your basketball credentials to anyone, but working in the men's game you can at least point to these experiences and say, "I've been there."

NL: I was at an NBA coaches symposium recently and Pat was telling the story up on the podium, about how Jerry West came to him and said, "You have a new player, Nancy Lieberman." And Pat was telling the audience that he said to Jerry, "I don't want her on my team."

Well, I was mortified. I just sat there, I was in the front row, and Pat looks at me and he tells the audience, "I didn't want her because she didn't fit what I thought in my mind to be my point guard. Quite frankly, I was judgmental and I did not want to coach her, a woman."

He went on to tell the story about my first practice. He said, "My guys beat the crap out of her. They are just knocking her all over the place for three hours. She doesn't say anything. She doesn't complain. She doesn't take herself out of any of the drills. As a matter of fact she tried to start a fight."

Well, that's true. I felt like some of the guys were pushing me a bit too hard, because they didn't want to play with a girl. Later in the practice, Pat tells us to go into a certain drill, but when he asked if any of the players knew it, none of the guys on the Lakers stepped up. Nobody raised their hand. And I said, "Coach, I know the drill."

And he looked at me kind of like a dog with his head turned. I knew he was thinking, "How the hell do you know this drill?" So I figured if I did the drill and I screwed up, he would curse me out. They would correct me after he corrected me, he would then allow me to go through repetition and then I would understand the drill. So my solution to getting on the court, being overmatched by these guys, was to actually be smart and understand it and be fearless so that's the back story.

And Pat told the audience, "I asked my coaches, 'Who is she? She acts like she's the best player on the team and she's not afraid of anything.'" Then he looks at me down in the front row at the symposium and said, "You made me fearless. Everything that I did from that point on, you made me fearless and Nancy, this is the truth, four days later you were my starting point guard. Everybody thinks that the first point guard I ever coached was Magic Johnson. You were my first point guard, and everybody on the team deferred to you."

To have that kind of backing in this game means everything.

CT: That's vintage Pat Riley. I want to fast forward a bit. I don't want to rehash the Detroit Shock story but obviously that was kind of a low point for you. How did you recover from that? Here you had the WNBA, it's arguably the first viable and stable women's professional league in the country at that time and you're out of a job. How did you manage that crisis in your career?

NL: Looking back, I truly consider my time with the Shock one of the great experiences of my life. When they hired me, they essentially handed me the franchise and said, "Build it," from the business to the player personnel to the coaching. I mean, trusting me with Mr. Davidson's franchise… In our first year we go 17 and 13. I believe that team still has the best expansion record in history of professional sports.

The second year we became the first expansion team to ever make the playoffs and then my third year we lost. We missed getting to the playoffs on the tie-breaker on the last day of the season in Orlando. After [that season], they gave me a three-year contract extension and I signed the extension but at the time my husband Tim had depression and I was really struggling with raising a four-year-old son. My husband was sick and here I am in Detroit. I remember thinking, "Can I do this? When do you have to put your family first?"

I was still broadcasting for ESPN and I was coaching and in three years I had done more than 800 speaking appearances. We were all over the place. But it was reflective of what our attendance was as an organization, so it meant that what we were doing was working. We were making money as a team. The biggest thrill for me was to tell Mr. Davidson we made money and we were in the black, not the red.

And then the Sports Illustrated article came out [with allegations about the affair with one of the players]. And the organization handled it really poorly. They reacted sort of off the cuff. I mean, you see how Pat Riley and Magic Johnson are inseparable, to this day, and the Shock could have been more supportive. I had a very disgruntled player, and she created this firestorm. I told her, "You're not hurting me by lying, but you are hurting women's sports as a whole." And I meant that.

Everybody's going to judge just how you should be with your players, and I think if you're a woman, you're at a definite disadvantage because everybody's going to say, "Well, you know, they're really tight so there must be something between them." Even when it's not true and obviously it's not most of the time. If an NBA guy or a professional football player, if they get arrested or charged with hitting their wives, the coaches or the front office will say, "Well, we really don't know what's going on yet. We'll just have to see how it plays out."

Well, my team captain wrote a letter to SI saying that the allegations weren't true, and still I was out of a job. There is a double standard and it makes you change because I deeply care about my players. You know what? Later, in 2009, when I was with my NBA D-League guys, when I was watching film with them at three in the morning...I mean I remember telling the wives of my assistant coaches, "This is an unusual situation where a woman is coaching guys. I might be in your husband's room at two in the morning. They might be in my room at two in the morning. You've got to really trust me here because I'd be a woman with a guy, you know what I'm saying..."

But I spent enormous amounts of time with my male players, taking them to lunch, sitting on the bus with them, getting to know their families, because I care. But I had to make sure I managed it because a woman coaching male players and working with male assistants was new and it was a first and I had to make sure that I handled things appropriately, with class and character. I told somebody a long time ago, "I'm not in control of my reputation but I'm always in control of my character." It's a shame it's an issue, but that's reality.

People are going to take shots at you. It's going to happen if you're in any sort of high-profile business. Unfortunately those things are going to happen and you just have to be stalwart and you've just got to be so strong. Even though you're hurt, you have to be really strong.

CT: During the midst of all that, or just on the heels of being fired by the Detroit Shock, you go back to Old Dominion and finish up your degree. Was that something that was important to you to do at the time and was it something that helped sort of pave the way for what you did in the next chapter of your life?

NL: It was important to me because every time I was going past Old Dominion and I'd see the uniforms hanging from the rafters… Sports is a two-way street. I always viewed myself as a professional even back at Old Dominion. They didn't give me a scholarship because I was a nice girl. They gave me a scholarship because I had talent to earn a scholarship.

I love that university so much that I just felt at that time a little cheated—not by the university, just by circumstances. I had to drop my hours my junior and senior year to go to the Olympic trials and the Pan Am trials so I missed my degree. And here I am teaching children about school and education and I couldn't back up what I was saying and that really bothered me.

I had been offered honorary degrees from three or four different universities but I would never do that because I just love Old Dominion. It meant so much to me in my development. So walking with my class, I think it was May 6th of 2000—that was unbelievable. What a great moment for me and my family, and yeah that process helped me move on.

CT: Now here you are breaking down barriers and pioneering yet again, working in the NBA Development League, first as a coach and now as an executive as well with a men's professional team. How did that come about?

NL: [Dallas Mavericks and Texas Legends President] Donnie [Nelson] came to me. I was at ESPN. I had been there 28 years when Donnie called me. We had maybe five or six meetings and he says, "I want you to coach my team." I said, "Donnie, you're going to get a lot of heat on this."

But he told me he believed I was the template of the kind of coach he wanted to have working his D-League players. He said, "You played in men's minor league basketball. You played for the Lakers. You're a lifer. You've been a women's coach, and you've been around the men's game your whole life. You're not afraid." He told me he had confidence in my ability to navigate the obstacles. It was really amazing, I'm so grateful to Donnie because it's a [major] decision and when Donnie's in your corner nobody can ever hurt you or harm you. He's so protective.

And I had so many coaches in the league who championed me. I have to tell you, I could not have done my job without that support. When we made the playoffs—the Legends had not had any teams make the playoffs before—I mean it's crazy... I had a real sense of accomplishment.

But then in my second year, I was starting to miss all of [my son] T.J.'s high school games. He never said anything to me but the D-League has a 52-game season, and he would say to me, "Ma, can you come see me play?" But I couldn't. There was always a conflict. We were always playing.

After the Mavericks won the NBA championship [in the spring of 2011], Donnie and I spoke and I was like, "Donny, I've got to be a mom. I've got to be in the stands for my son's senior year." So I stepped down as coach, and Donnie being Donnie and having such an amazing heart, he offered me the position of assistant GM.

CT: So what's next for you, Nancy? I mean where do you see your career going from here?

NL: My goal is to coach in the NBA. I'd like to be an assistant in the NBA. I'm a basketball lifer. I'm intimately involved in the game. Being around the guys on the Thunder and the Legends, I would love to have an opportunity to coach on that next level. It would mean everything to me.

Author's note: Soon after this conversation, Nancy was hired as an assistant coach by the Sacramento Kings of the NBA.

Key Messages from Nancy Lieberman

Assess the crisis. When Nancy took over as coach of the NBA DL's Texas Legends, it wasn't exactly a crisis, but she knew from her past experiences as a woman trying out with the Los Angeles Lakers and as a coach and executive with the Detroit Shock in the WNBA—where her tenure didn't end well—that there would be issues for her as a woman coaching men. Rather than pretend these issues didn't exist, Nancy considered them and took them head-on. In the end, her proactiveness served her well, and positioned her to take what she hopes will be the next step—working in the NBA.

"You can't control your reputation, but you can control your character." This may have been the best comment from Nancy. Managers cannot worry about what others around them think. They have to act, and do so in a way that reflects their values and character.

Draw from past experiences. As Nancy continues to pioneer new trails as first a coach and then an executive in a men's professional sports league, she is able to use her experiences with the Los Angeles Lakers and legendary coach Pat Riley to find common ground with the players in her charge. As the old saying goes, "Experience is a hard teacher," but life's difficulties are meaningless if we don't learn from them. Nancy's outlook on her time with the Detroit Shock is a prime example of that.

Find a mentor. Nancy's friendship with Dick Schaap proved invaluable as she navigated the waters as the face of her sport at only 18 years of age. As Nancy tells it, Dick provided her with guidance in terms of how to act as a professional—and on what to say and how to say it. All leaders and managers need a mentor in times of crisis, someone to serve as a sounding board for ideas, for insights into how to handle personal matters or address workplace issues. It can be a supervisor or a colleague at a similar level, either within or outside the organization, and the relationship can be a two-way street. But it is vital.

Chapter Two

Lou Vairo: Coach, USA Hockey

Lou Vairo is a hockey lifer. Born and raised in Brooklyn, he grew up watching the sport at the old Madison Square Garden, cheering for his beloved New York Rangers. He went on to play and coach the sport, becoming one of the most well-known bench managers in American hockey.

Starting in the American junior ranks in the mid-1970s, Vairo rose up quickly to become head coach of the National Junior Team, a position he held for three years, from 1979-82. He guided the team again in 2003.

Although Vairo served as an assistant coach with the New Jersey Devils of the National Hockey League (NHL) in the mid-1980s, he is perhaps best known for his work with the U.S. Men's National Team program. Vairo served as an assistant coach for the famous "Miracle on Ice" team that won Olympic gold in Lake Placid in 1980—considered by some to be the most significant event in modern U.S. sports history—and for the team that captured a silver medal during the 2002 Winter Olympics in Salt Lake City. He also served as head coach of the team on several occasions, leading the team in the annual World Ice Hockey Championships first from 1980-83, and then again from 2000-2003.

Barring his brief time in the NHL, his three-year stint as head coach of HC Milano Saimo in Italy and one year as head coach of the Dutch National Team, Vairo has been affiliated with USA Hockey, in some capacity, since 1979. He presently serves as Director, Special Projects for the organization, and he has been credited with implementing its Diversity Task Force, a program that is designed to bring hockey to inner city and minority communities, and with helping create its Select Player Development Camps, which are modeled after similar programs overseas and designed to train and develop young players. Many within the sport believe the camps, and the USA National Team Development Program in Michigan have been vital in developing players in this country, expanding and deepening the talent pool for junior and college programs and ultimately, of course, the national team.

In 2000, Vairo received the Lester B. Patrick Award in recognition of his service to hockey in the U.S. and, in 2010, he was recognized by the International Ice Hockey Federation (IIHF) as the recipient of the Paul Loicq Award, which is named after a long-serving president of the IIHF and is the organization's highest honor.

Yes, Vairo has done a lot in American hockey, including serving as a head coach with the U.S. Men's National and National Junior teams on several occasions, but he faced by far his most difficult challenge in that role during the 1984 Winter Olympics in Sarajevo, in the former Yugoslavia. After "the Miracle" in 1980, expectations were high, but USA Hockey was hardly the top-notch, well-heeled organization it is today. Even with the success in Lake Placid, sponsorship money was still hard to come by and budgets were tight. In addition, this was 14 years before NHL players were allowed to participate in the Games. As in Lake Placid, most of the players were in their late teens or early twenties, and drawn from the American amateur and collegiate ranks.

So how did Vairo manage the media-fueled frenzy surrounding his team of young players? Well, he took time out of his busy schedule to speak to us from his office in Colorado Springs and tell us about how he and his players managed the crises associated with such lofty expectations and share a few words of wisdom for young managers and coaches, both inside and outside the sports world.

Crunch Time: First of all, what was it like following in the footsteps of the legendary Herb Brooks, head coach of the 1980 "Miracle" team, and dealing with the high expectations for the 1984 team that came with the success in Lake Placid?

Lou Vairo: Well, being an assistant on that team was one of the greatest times in my life. I consider it my second greatest achievement, with serving in the military being the first. To be on the staff, working upstairs and sharing my observations with [assistant coach] Craig [Patrick] and Herb was just an amazing experience. Such a great group of players and coaches.

So, I want to be clear, I was not bitter or anything at all about following up on that. It never even crossed my mind. I also wasn't nervous about it. I knew what we accomplished in Lake Placid was special, and in 1984 we had a different group, a younger group.

I had been serving as the head coach of the men's team [at the World Championships] for the three years before the 1984 Games, and I was on the search committee for the coach for the 1984 Olympic team. A lot of people don't know this but we actually had a hard time finding a coach for that 1984 team. We offered the job to a number of college and pro coaches but they all turned us down. The program was different back then. It was a huge commitment, and it meant they would have to leave their full-time jobs. And we didn't have the kind of money back then to encourage them to come over.

I was supposed to go to Calgary in 1983 to work as an assistant with the Flames, with the great "Badger" Bob [Johnson]. He had left the University of Wisconsin to go up to the NHL, and later went on to win a Stanley Cup with Pittsburgh. But the USA Hockey search committee asked me to put my NHL plans on hold and step in to be head coach. I am fully committed to USA Hockey, so I decided to do it, and I don't regret it at all. We had a tough task, and we didn't do as well as we had hoped, but that 1984 team was a great group of players. I loved coaching them.

CT: You've really been around to see the growth of USA Hockey. I mean, people who follow the sport wouldn't believe that the program would have a problem finding a coach…

LV: Yeah, that's true, but in those days, things were different. We didn't have the money we do today, and we didn't have the youth development program. But we've always had great people, from the players to the coaches, the volunteers and the executives. We've been able to build off the success of the 1980 team and grow the program and the sport here in the U.S.

CT: But a lot of people probably didn't know the organizational challenges you had back then, even after the "Miracle on Ice." So maybe some of the expectations for the 1984 team on the outside were unfair…

LV: Unfair to the players, maybe. I'll tell you, that 1984 team worked just as hard as that 1980 team. They were great group of players. Chris Chelios, who went on to have a Hall of Fame career in the NHL, played hurt that whole tournament. Patty LaFontaine, I think, also battled injuries. Paul Guay, too.

But for us as coaches, we had high expectations, too. I've always believed that you only have one winner. In a way, the whole Olympic set-up—with gold, silver and bronze medals—is kind of fake. To me, there's gold—the winner—and nothing else.

That wasn't our message to the players, though. We told them to play hard, to have fun and to represent their country with pride, and I think they did that. I was proud of that team then, and I still am now.

CT: Still, you must have been disappointed with the seventh-place finish...

LV: Damn right. But as the coach of that team, the leader, I take responsibility for that. Not those players. Remember, these were nineteen- and twenty-year-old kids. I remember seeing them line up in the tunnel to take the ice before our first game in that Olympics, and I could see the fear in their eyes. They were scared. I think they heard the expectations from the outside and, even if they didn't, they knew what had had happened in 1980—who didn't?—and they didn't want to be seen as failures.

I think my only regret about that team, or maybe my whole career, is that I wasn't able to get them to not play scared. And you can't play any sport scared. I tried, but I guess I failed as a leader on that.

CT: Well, you played in a tough group, with Canada, Czechoslovakia and Finland. The Czechs won a bronze medal, and the Soviets and the Swedes, who had a much easier group, won gold and silver, respectively. There's no shame in where you finished among those teams.

LV: No there isn't, but a lot of people who don't know hockey don't know that. Look, I just look at the roster of players we had in 1984. A bunch of them went on to have great careers in the NHL. Guys like Chelios and LaFontaine are Hall of Famers. And a bunch of them were team captains in their careers, or became coaches themselves. We had a lot of great leaders on that team; a lot of character.

CT: Speaking of that, hockey truly is a sport about leadership and character, because it's so physical and difficult to play. You've coached players at all levels, and at all ages. Is it harder to find leaders on a young team like that 1984 team?

LV: No. Leaders show themselves to be leaders. You watch guys like Chelios, LaFontaine, [Ed] Olczyk, and you can see they're leaders. Phil Verchota is a leader…

CT: All great managers say they need good people around them. So how do you recognize those leaders?

LV: You watch how they are with their teammates, how they prepare for games, or even practices. You also see how they handle pressure, or adversity. It's easy to be a strong leader when things are going good, it's how you lead in times of trouble that matters. Every manager or coach needs to find those guys who show leadership and character in bad times.

CT: Speaking of preparation, you are known for it. You were one of the first coaches in North American hockey to travel overseas and learn European systems. Talk about that.

LV: I took a lot of heat for it back then. A lot of people in the game didn't think there was a lot to learn from the Europeans. I was fortunate enough early on in my career to meet Anatoli Tarasov, the so-called "father" of Russian hockey. Back then, under the Soviets, the Russian hockey federation had some of the best training techniques around and I learned a lot from him. I call him "Professor." He is probably my biggest mentor.

CT: Did having Tarasov's support and counsel help you in your career?

LV: Everyone needs a mentor, someone to seek out for advice. As a coach, you don't always have all the answers.

CT: How did Tarasov help you and, indirectly, help USA Hockey?

LV: He told me early on, "Lou don't copy other people. Learn from them and develop your own style." So that's what I've done. I watched how the Soviets trained, how they practiced, how they set up their teams, how they developed players. Now, there were a lot of things we couldn't do. Remember, they were a dictatorship back then. The government could force players to play, force them to train, keep them isolated from friends and family. Obviously, we couldn't do that here.

But we could take some of their practice and training styles and use them. A little bit of what we do through our National Team Development Program (NTDP) and the Select Development Camps comes from the Soviet approach, probably, although I don't know how much we want to admit that [laughs]. Now, our best young players go into the NTDP, they live there, go to school there, and learn from the best coaches in the country. We manage their training, conditioning, their nutrition, and we identify good, young players earlier. If you want to compete, you have to be able to do that, and now we do. In the seventies and eighties, even earlier, the Soviets and others were already doing that.

People just assume we were doing that when we won gold in 1980, but we weren't. Not even close. Those were college players. We didn't have the set-up we do now until the mid-nineties.

CT: And now you're around to teach younger coaches...

LV: Well, maybe [laughs]. I'm not sure I have much to offer.

CT: Come on, former national team coach... You've seen a lot in your career.

LV: I'm still learning. I watched those New York Yankees teams in the nineties, watched how Joe Torre managed them, how the players handled themselves. [Derek] Jeter is the best Yankee I ever saw; well, maybe Yogi [Berra] was. I mean, those guys are winners. And I saw [Mickey] Mantle and [Joe] DiMaggio at the end. And the manager? Torre. Talk about class.

In all sports—hell, in life—you see so many great characters, great leaders. The key is to watch them and learn. Study them. See how they prepare, how they manage their players, how they manage tough situations, and try to take a piece of that and use it.

Tarasov and the Russians were supposed to be our enemies, right? But I knew that they did certain things well, and I knew we could learn from them. Tarasov was an amazing man, and an amazing coach.

CT: So sports can be a good life education?

LV: I think so. I know I've been around sports my whole life and I feel like I've learned a lot about life through sports. Serving my country was also big. I believe everyone should have to serve in the military, at least for one year. Bring back the draft! I'm not saying everyone needs to see combat. They can be in the military and do community service or public projects. In fact, I think if everyone had to serve in the military we'd have less war. People would have a better understanding of it.

Mandatory service would give everyone an idea of what it means to serve, to commit to something, to do something for your country, your community. You have to be committed to what you're doing in life, your family, your community, your work. That commitment is what gives you the strength to get through anything.

CT: You mentioned great Yankees before... Who is the best player to come through USA Hockey?

LV: Oh man! Tough question [laughs]! God, I loved them all. Chelios, LaFontaine, [goalie Tom] Barrasso, [Mike] Modano, [Keith] Tkachuk, [Mike] Richter, [Brian] Leetch. The guys on that

1980 team don't get enough credit for what great players they were. Everyone talks about how they were young, amateur, college players—boys playing against men from Europe. But there were some great players on that team. [Mark] Pavelich, [Mark] Johnson, [Dave] Christian. Rob McClanahan. Mike Ramsey. Kenny Morrow. The captain, [Mike] Eurozione, wasn't the most talented guy, but no one worked harder. And he was a great leader.

CT: You can't give me one guy?

LV: Alright, alright [laughs]. Neil Broten. Again, not the most talented to ever come through. But a great, great player. Easy to coach. Great character. Worked as hard as anyone. Great teammate. Very committed to USA Hockey. Nobody wore the jersey with more pride.

CT: What's next for Lou Vairo?

LV: Who knows [laughs]? I'm happy where I'm at here, at USA Hockey. The program has grown so much. Now, we're in contention in every tournament we enter, and we have great young players coming up. We have the best coaches in the world now. And the board of directors is great… all the volunteers… The program is in the best shape it's ever been in. It's a great place to be. But even if we were still struggling for money, still scrambling to get facilities or struggling to find players and coaches, I'd still be working at it. Like I said, being committed to what you do is so important; it'll help get you through anything.

Author's note: Lou Vairo may be humble, as well as self-effacing. But, make no mistake, he is as important a leader in USA Hockey as there ever has been. A coach on some of the most successful national teams in the program, and an innovator who has helped revolutionize how it prepares players for international competition, Lou's legacy will endure for as long as the puck is dropped and one of the teams playing is wearing red, white and blue.

Crunch Time

Key Messages from Lou Vairo

Don't fear your competition. Learn from them. U.S.-Russian relations were hardly warm in the 1970s and 1980s, when Lou Vairo and Anatoli Tarasov became close friends. In fact, as Lou notes, he took some heat from his colleagues at USA Hockey for the relationship. However, hockey was common ground, and the two men learned a lot from one another. Tarasov's approach served as one of the building blocks for USA Hockey's National Team Development Program (NTDP). Established in 1996, the NTDP has trained and developed players in their teens and graduated numerous top performers. It has placed the U.S. national team program on equal footing with some of the best in the world, and a lot of the program's facets can be traced back to the exchange of ideas between Lou and Tarasov.

Be your own manager; don't try to be the manager who came before you. Lou could have viewed following on the heels of the legendary Herb Brooks and the 1980 Miracle on Ice as head coach of the 1984 Olympic team as a source of pressure. Instead, he saw it as an opportunity. As a competitor, he wasn't pleased with the team's performance in 1984, but he knows the players and coaches still did USA Hockey and the country as a whole proud through their hard work and character. Lou never tried to be Brooks. He simply tried to be Lou Vairo. New managers will often hear things like, "That's not how we usually do it," from staff in the initial period they're in charge. It's important not to succumb to the pressure to do what your predecessor did, and to stick with the approach you believe is the right course of action, and the one that makes you most comfortable.

Identify good leaders and good characters on your team, who step up in times of adversity. Managers cannot go it alone in times of crisis. They need the support of lower level staff and managers to succeed. But not everyone can thrive under pressure. Lou looked at how players on his teams treated their teammates and performed in all situations, both good and bad. The true leaders, he says, were the ones who continued to display grit and character — and class — when the going got rough.

Chapter Three
Bruce Baumgartner: Olympic Wrestling Gold Medal Winner and World Champion

Olympic gold medal winner Bruce Baumgartner was the face of American wrestling—and perhaps the most successful amateur wrestler in the world – for much of the 1980s and early 1990s. So it's no wonder that the sport turned to him, along with a few other leaders, as it faced its biggest crisis in the modern era.

In 2013, the International Olympic Committee (IOC) voted to eliminate wrestling from the Summer Games for 2020 and beyond, citing declining interest from corporate sponsors and fans. It didn't help that youth development programs had been experiencing declining enrollment for decades, or that many U.S. colleges were dropping the sport on the intercollegiate level because, among other reasons, it is not seen as a revenue producer.

The IOC vote served as a wake-up call for wrestling, which not only dates back to the first modern-day Olympiad in 1896 but the first documented sporting games in 708 B.C. Leadership was changed at FILA, wrestling's governing body in the immediate aftermath of the vote and, with USA Wrestling taking a lead role, a "Committee for the Preservation of Olympic Wrestling" was formed. The committee proposed a number of rule changes, which were enacted for the 2016 Games. Two new weight classes were added on the women's side, improving gender equity (an issue cited by the IOC) and several "tweaks," as Baumgartner puts it, were made to make the sport more exciting. Here in the U.S., a grassroots campaign was launched to increase youth participation and encourage colleges to preserve and/or restore wrestling programs.

So far, the efforts seem to have worked. Several colleges have restored intercollegiate wrestling programs, and interest in the sport is growing once again. Most notably, the IOC reversed its decision and voted to return wrestling to the Olympic lineup, albeit provisionally, for 2020 and 2024.

The achievement is only the latest feather in Baumgartner's proverbial cap. After becoming a champion as a collegian at Indiana State University (ISU), he won Olympic gold twice—first in 1984 and then again, in a bit of a surprise, in 1992 at age 32. He also won silver in 1988 and, again in a bit of surprise, bronze in 1996 in Atlanta at age 36. He medaled at the sports World Championships nine times, including three golds (with one in his last competition at the Worlds in 1995), and medaled four times (three golds, one silver) at the Pan American Games. He has since been inducted in the ISU Athletics Hall of Fame, the Missouri Valley Conference Hall of Fame, the U.S. Olympic Hall of Fame, the National Wrestling Hall of Fame, and the FILA International Wrestling Hall of Fame.

After retiring from the sport in 1998, Baumgartner went on to become a coach and administrator. He serves on the Board of Directors for USA Wrestling and, after serving as the school's wrestling coach for 13 years, he now works as the Director of Athletics for Edinboro University of Pennsylvania. As both an athlete and administrator, Baumgartner has wrestled (sorry) with challenges head-on, and come out with arms raised high in victory. Crunch Time spoke to him at his office in Erie, Pa.

Crunch Time: You've devoted your entire life to sports in general and wrestling in particular. What did you think when you first heard about the IOC's decision to eliminate the sport from the Olympics in 2020?

Bruce Baumgartner: Well, I think that it was a shock to the wrestling world. Literally a week or so before [the vote], our sources domestically and even some of the Russian wrestling sources, we all felt that wrestling was going to be safe and it was going to be some other sport, modern pentathlon maybe, but not wrestling, that would be dropped. That Tuesday or Monday morning after the meeting we were all shocked. We all knew that the IOC executive committee meeting was happening but, again, the sources throughout the world were saying it was not going to be wrestling that took the fall.

CT: Definitely a crisis for the sport...

BB: I think it was. USA Wrestling, a lot of very smart business people, a lot of influential people both financially and politically, we got together and met, via conference call mostly, every Saturday after that and each of us took on a different responsibility in an effort to save the sport. There were a lot of different fronts that the fight was fought on. When you analyze why wrestling was removed, it's not that dissimilar from why some companies lose their edge.

CT: Can you describe, briefly, some of the key changes proposed by the Committee for the Preservation of Olympic Wrestling and what changes were ultimately instituted?

BB: Well, first, we partnered with similar committees in Russia, Iran and Japan, and though we were not all best friends politically we were unified in our love for the sport. Ultimately, I'd say the U.S. and Russia took the biggest leaps in terms of effort and changes.

We started to modernize the sport. We worked on promoting the sport on Facebook and Twitter and getting it promoted better on TV. We also sponsored a number of exhibition events in places like L.A., Aspen and New York, at Grand Central Station. These events were designed to familiarize more people with the sport and its rules, to make it more fan-friendly, to get people interested and excited.

CT: Well, clearly what you did worked. What do you think was the key?

BB: We brought in people who are good on social media and marketing, and we found some people who are very good at organizational administration and organizational realignment. They performed an organizational review to create a more efficient organization. A lot of people came together and I think that's important when a crisis hits. Sometimes you need a different perspective, new ideas.

CT: Were there any parallels with your own career and could you draw upon those experiences in your effort to save the sport?

BB: In my wrestling career, I'm winning gold medals in 1988, 1989, in 1990, but then in 1991 I don't do very well. I didn't medal at the Worlds for the first time in eight years. Well, I worked hard, I did everything right but I didn't change, I didn't keep up to date. I didn't stay with the times per se. I got complacent.

Up until 1990, I won medals in international competition. Then I was the eighth and last person to qualify to represent the U.S. in the 1992 Olympics. I was devastated. But by then, everybody knew what Bruce Baumgartner was going to do. Everybody knew my strengths and my weaknesses. I needed to change. And I did. Over a year or so, I just got better. If you look at my 1992 Olympics, I had one point scored on me, I think I beat the returning world champion by eight points, the returning Olympic champion by three points. In the finals, I beat the reigning bronze medalist by eight or nine points.

I knew I needed to make some changes. I surrounded myself with good people. I got good coaches, good workout partners, nutritionists, sports psychologists. I didn't train any harder for the 1992 Olympics than I did the 1991 World Championships, I trained smarter and surrounded myself with better people and I was able to win the Olympics in somewhat of a dominant fashion, beating the returning Olympic champion and the returning World champion.

And I think that's a little bit what happened to the wrestling world. My wrestling career is proof that you have to stay flexible, you have to stay up to date and you need to surround yourself with good people. With wrestling, we became complacent as a sport. We let our rules become complex and not fan- or wrestler-friendly. We allowed our international governing body to become full of administrators who were not focused on keeping up with the changes in the sports world. Wrestling didn't have good leadership when it crashed. Now I think we have good leadership.

CT: Can you talk about some of the changes you made heading into the 1992 Olympic Games?

BB: Well, one of the deficiencies I think I had was I didn't have a freestyle workout partner. So I had a fellow freestyle wrestler— Mike Fusilli—come and live with me, from November of 1991 right through until the Olympics. Mike was the sixth- or seventh-ranked American at the time, and he had been as high as fourth at one time, so he was a great training partner, someone who could challenge me. Training with him everyday really forced me to look at my technique and see where I could make adjustments.

Then I consulted with nutritionists to work on my diet. Now, I wasn't doing a ton wrong at the time; my diet was good. But sometimes it's not major changes that make a difference. It's just doing something a little bit differently. If I was going to rate myself on a scale from maybe one to 10, 10 being perfect eating habits, I was maybe a five at the time. Well, I got myself to an eight or a nine. I would never profess to have a perfect diet [laughs].

So what you have to do is if you see a weakness, you have to improve it and you have to overcome that weakness somewhere else. I went and I talked to coaches on some new techniques and new holds I should learn that could fit into my style without retraining myself how to wrestle totally. I wanted to give my opponents a different enough look that my old techniques and my new techniques would augment each other to be more successful.

I worked out a little bit smarter, probably a little bit harder but I wouldn't say much harder. At 31 years old, I was still maybe training like I was 28, not a huge difference, but enough. And as you see in the NBA and NFL and other sports, you need to evolve your training as you get older, and I started to do that heading into the 1992 Games. I talked to coaches and I went to a sports psychologist to do some affirmation and learn some relaxation techniques—again not what I would call major overhauls but just augmenting what I did.

CT: Do you think you would have pursued all of those approaches if you hadn't had a disappointing finish at the Worlds in 1991, where you didn't medal? Was that kind of a kick in the pants that you needed or were you thinking about making adjustments anyway?

BB: No, I felt like I was wrestling really well heading into the Worlds. I trained hard. I did a lot of things right. I knew I just needed to make little improvements. When you improve the four, five or six different facets of your training and preparation—your strength, your endurance, your conditioning, your technique, your defense—and you improve each one just a little bit, it adds up.

So I don't know that I would have done it had I done better at the Worlds. If you look at my career, I won Olympics in 1992, the Worlds in 1993, I was silver in 1994, 1995 I got a gold, and then in Atlanta I got a bronze and I was 35 years old.

CT: So you certainly responded to the crisis in your career, and overcame it. Would you say that the crisis is over for wrestling now that it's been reinstated or is it really still paramount upon you and other leaders within the sport to continue to grow the sport, get more young people involved in it and not just in the U.S. but maybe across the world?

BB: I think it is absolutely essential that we learn from our mistakes, or even if you don't call it a mistake, you learn from your past. You do not want the past to repeat. I hope every time that USA Wrestling, and I know we're working on it domestically, because a lot of this stuff takes a lot of money... It's not cheap. But I hope every time we do a major event, we do it first class, we make something that the fans feel good about, that the wrestlers feel good about. The wrestling fanatic will be there. Wrestling needs to, as all sports do, except for your major probably three or four Olympic sports, to court the viewer. They need to have people following our athletes on Twitter, on Facebook, on Snapchat, all the other social media.

You know, [American wrestler and gold-medal winner at the 2012 Summer Olympics in London] Jordan Burroughs now has an unbelievable amount of people that follow him on Twitter. Well that's what we need to keep doing as a sport. And there are minor things as well. We need to keep evolving the rules, keep them understandable, keep them simple, keep them media friendly. The first couple years I was wrestling internationally the sport had great rules but your matches could be in overtime six or seven minutes. Nobody wants to watch a zero-zero or a 1-0 match that goes 18 minutes, and the people who broadcast the Olympics know that. So it's imperative that the sport continues to evolve.

Now our World Championships next year are in Las Vegas, so we need to be in places like Las Vegas, New York, Tokyo, Istanbul and Moscow, in big, big cities where we can put a good show on to try to make it appealing for the media, make it appealing for the fans, make it interesting and exciting for the kids that may want to wrestle one day to watch. We need to continue to make improvements in the overall sport every day, in every competition. I don't think any sport is safe if they don't do that.

CT: Now that you have been an administrator for a while, I am sure you have an even better sense of that...

BB: You're right, and it's funny, I sort of got here by accident. When I was still wrestling competitively, I was also the assistant to the head wrestling coach at Edinboro University and when I retired from wrestling I started to get into athletic administration. Eventually, I became the athletic director at Edinboro University and I've been the AD now for over 15 years now, dealing with a wide variety of different issues.

CT: I know you went to Indiana State so how did you end up at Edinboro?

BB: When I went to college, I wanted to be an industrial arts teacher. My dad was a bus mechanic and I kind of liked wood shop, mechanical drawing, metal shop and auto shop classes that they had at my high school [in Haledon, New Jersey] and I figured it would be really good to teach, maybe coach a little wrestling along the way. So I went to Indiana State and got my undergraduate degree in industrial arts education and then went to Oklahoma State as a graduate assistant and trained for the Olympics, from 1982 to 1984, and got my degree in industrial education with specialization in adult education.

In May of 1984, before the Olympics, Oklahoma State had a coaching change and I was out of a job. Mike DeAna, from the University of Iowa, got the head-coaching job at Edinboro. I wrestled against him in college and with him in the Olympic program so I knew him pretty well. Anyway, the Athletic Director (AD) at Edinboro at the time called me in for an interview and he liked me so I got the job as an assistant. They were bringing the program up from Division II to Division I so it was an exciting time to be here. Originally, my wife and I were going to stay in Erie for maybe two or three years, or maybe until I retired from competitive wrestling, but we fell in love with the place and I've been here ever since. I was the head coach of the wrestling team from 1990 through 1997 and then I became AD.

CT: Wrestling programs were getting dropped at a number of schools in 1990s and early 2000s, but recently a few have announced plans to bring the sport back. As an AD now, what is your perspective on that?

BB: I think Edinboro has a pretty strong program right now. We have probably the best coach in the country in Tim Flynn, who is a Penn State grad. My predecessor here was from Iowa, and I wrestled at Indiana State and coached at Oklahoma State. So there are a number of schools where the programs are strong and there's a tradition in wrestling.

But people like me and Tim Flynn are not going to be here forever. As new blood, new leaders come in, they can't become complacent. If they do, I think almost any program is in trouble, or could be in trouble. Nobody knows what is going to happen with the NCAA in Division I basketball and football going forward, and whatever does happen will trickle down and affect the other sports. You have conference realignment, antitrust lawsuits, a movement for unionization of student-athletes. Wrestling may be a relatively small sport compared to football and basketball, but it needs to have a voice in all of this, and it needs to have people on the watch, making sure that the sport's future is safe.

CT: As an AD, have you faced in major crises at Edinboro? If so, what has been your approach to managing them?

BB: Well, thankfully, we've not really had any what I would call major crises but we've had some bad things happen, athletes with academic problems, for example. I like to think I'm a thoughtful person, a person who acts rationally, not based on emotion. Now I'm not a doctor or the President of the United States, somebody who is making life or death decisions, so maybe I have it a bit easier than a lot of managers. But I've always thought that the best thing to do is keep your emotions in check. Stay level-headed.

What happens a lot of times when you first get hit with something negative or a crisis situation is that you may get upset or angry or think, "Why me?" But, in the end, that stuff doesn't matter to the people affected by the decisions you make. In my case as an AD, again I'm not making life-changing decisions, but I am hopefully looking to make positive change in the lives of the young men and women who go to school here and play sports here. If my blood pressure goes up and I start screaming and hollering when there is a problem, it doesn't make that problem go away any quicker or that issue get resolved any quicker.

Just like with the committee that was formed to preserve wrestling, I find that tackling problems is done best when you have a group of people working together to fix them. And we try to do that here. We'll work together as a team of administrators, gather information from the principals involved in the problem—the athletes or coaches affected—and bring in smart people to help you make a decision based on the information you have. And once you make a decision, you move forward with a defined plan, and you stick with it, assuming it's the right way to go, or you change it, again with input from key stakeholders, based on new information.

It can't be about the emotion of it and I think that's where sometimes some pretty smart people wind up not necessarily helping in a crisis, because they respond by acting before they have all the facts, by acting when they're in a highly emotional state. Sometimes you just have to take a breath and get all the information. And you can't do it alone.

I don't care whether you're a coach, an athlete, you know, the President of the United States, a Fortune 500 chairman of the board, president or CEO, you need to have good people around you to bounce ideas off of. That's where I've been fortunate in my wrestling career and I think that's why I'm fortunate at Edinboro. We have a very good staff, both coaches and athletic administrators.

Key Messages from Bruce Baumgartner

When faced with a crisis, form a team. When the International Olympic Committee voted to drop wrestling as a sport from the Summer Olympic games in 2020 and 2024, wrestling leaders worldwide joined together to address the crisis. Bruce Baumgartner was part of that team. Bruce has expertise as a wrestler, and as an athletics administrator, but by his own admission he does not have the skills needed to rescue the sport on his own.

The story is illustrative of the fact that sometimes the best thing a leader can do in a time of crisis is ask for help. Leaders don't need to know everything; and they need to admit when they don't. When crisis hits, form a team to meet the challenge—include members from different departments and/or backgrounds who have the skills or expertise needed to solve the problem. The Committee to Preserve Wrestling featured current and former wrestlers, coaches, administrators and executives with experience in marketing, finance and management. All of these were important in its successful efforts to have the sport restored to the Summer Olympics.

Keep emotions in check. As Bruce points out, human nature often leads all of us to ask, "Why me?" whenever something bad happens, in life or in business. It is important to fight this impulse. As Bruce notes, "screaming and hollering" and looking for someone to blame ultimately doesn't solve a problem or address a crisis. "Stay level-headed," as Bruce says. This sets a good example for those in your charge and enables you to keep your head clear and think of actual solutions to the problem at hand.

Be prepared for change by being prepared to change. If there is one lesson to learn from wrestling's fall (or at least stumble) from grace, it is that avoiding complacency can help you avoid problems. Organizations can avert some crises simply by being nimble and open to change. Companies with long, successful track records don't achieve that by doing business the same way year in and year out—they change to meet the changing demands of the times. Or better yet, they change to stay ahead of these changing demands.

Crunch Time

Crunch Time

Chapter Four
Mark Gubicza: World Series Champion

For years, Mark Gubicza didn't wear his World Series ring. He wasn't trying to make a statement. It just didn't feel right to him.

After all, Gubicza earned the ring as a member of the 1985 Kansas City Royals title-winning team, and the former pitcher with 132 Major League wins to his name has been working as a broadcaster for the Los Angeles Angels of Anaheim, the team with which he finished his career, for much of the 2000s. He feels wearing the ring with a Royals' logo would be disrespectful to his current employer.

But Gubicza is also a humble guy, in spite of his 14-year, big-league career, which included two All-Star Game appearances. He is quick to point out that he was only in his second year in the Major Leagues when the Royals won the 1985 Series, and he served as the fifth starter in a five-man rotation that, statistically, produced one of the best seasons in recent baseball history. In fact, Gubicza was, somewhat famously, left out of the team's pitching rotation for the postseason that year. However, there is hardly any shame in being ranked behind the likes of Charlie Liebrandt, Bret Saberhagen, Danny Jackson and Bud Black. Liebrandt finished the 1985 season with a 17-9 win-loss record and a superb 2.69 earned run average

(ERA). Saberhagen was even better, with a 20-6 record and a 2.87 ERA. Jackson and Black also finished with double-digit win totals.

So Gubicza left the ring at home—that is until former Royals teammate and Hall-of-Famer George Brett urged him to wear it proudly during Kansas City's run to the 2014 World Series (which they eventually lost to the San Francisco Giants). Brett reminded Gubicza that he was a valuable contributor to the 1985 team, with 14 regular-season wins—and a key performance in the pinch during that phenomenal postseason run.

Gubicza draws on lessons learned from that 1985 season, as well as in his personal life, to provide some keen insights on crisis management. He arguably was key to that Royals team facing down a crisis during the American League Championship Series, and he faced his own personal crisis, years later, due to the illness of one of his children. He talked with Crunch Time from his home in Southern California, just after the conclusion of the 2014 World Series.

Crunch Time: So you went years without wearing your World Series ring from 1985. Was that just out of respect for the Angels organization or was there something else behind that?

Mark Gubicza: Mostly that. You know, we won it early in my career. It was only my second year in the big leagues and I wore it pretty religiously for a long period of time. Then when I was traded over to the Angels I put it away. Not that I was mad at the Royals or anything like that. It's that I just felt that I went to a new organization and that I owed my focus to them as an organization, both at that point playing, although I didn't play that long or all that successfully for the Angels, and then eventually as a broadcaster.

When I started doing the pre- and post-game shows for both the [Los Angeles] Dodgers and the Angels, for Fox Sports Net at that point, back in 2000, I didn't wear it regularly. And for the past eight years I've been doing every game for the Angels, and it just didn't seem right to wear it. The Angels wouldn't have cared but I just felt that my focus should be on them. I didn't want Angels fans coming up to me and saying, "Why are you wearing a Royals ring when you work for the Angels?" I would have good answers for that normally [laughs] but I figured, "You know what? My focus is going to be strictly with the Angels and helping the fans enjoy and learn something every game."

CT: You were a young player on that Royals team, only in your second year, and you were the fifth starter in arguably one of the better five-man rotations in recent memory. When I read somewhere that you didn't wear your ring much, I thought, "I hope he's not doing that because he doesn't think he deserves to..."

MG: No, no, nothing like that. Though when George [Brett] made that comment to me during the Royals' run to the 2014 World Series, their first appearance in the Series since 1985, I was like, "Alright, I'm wearing it for him the rest of the time through the team's run." So yeah, it made me feel good when he said that, and it was a reminder that when you win in baseball, you win as a team.

And at the time, as a second-year guy, I understood the decision [Royals' manager] Dick Howser and [pitching coach] Gary Blaylock made about our rotation in the postseason. I mean, you had Charlie [Liebrandt], Bret [Saberhagen] and [Danny] Jackson as our top three, and then me and Buddy [Black] would be there if needed. And our coaching staff was smart in that they told Buddy and I to stay ready. They said, "Let's see how the series turns out."

CT: Right. And then you're called upon to pitch Game 6 of the League Championship Series against Toronto, and you could argue that your team was in crisis mode at that point.

MG: For sure. We fell behind in the LCS, losing the first two games. Then we come back and win Game 3, but lost again in Game 4. Danny Jackson pitches a shutout in Game 5, but we're still down 3-2.

When we got to Toronto for Game 6, I remember Dick Howser pulled me into his office [at the stadium] and said, "Hey, by the way, you're pitching Game 6."

CT: As a second-year player, were you nervous?

MG: At first. When Dick told me, I was like, "Whoa… Am I ready?" But then I thought, "Alright. Perfect." And it helped that, as soon as the other guys found out, George Brett, our leader, came right up to me in the clubhouse before the game and he goes, "Hey man. This is awesome, man. Hey, the bottom line is we win, you go out there and you deal, we play Game 7. If not we have a tee time the next day on the golf course." So that relaxed me a bit.

Since we won Game 5, I already had my dad, my uncle and one of my American Legion team baseball coaches coming up to Toronto and they were all staying in my hotel room the night before Game 6. Little did I know I was actually going to be pitching and starting the game the next night. So when you have three older men in your room and they're all snoring about as loud as somebody chopping and sawing logs, I didn't even get any sleep the night before the biggest game of my life to that point [laughs].

CT: So you find out you're starting the game… How did you mentally prepare for the start?

MG: Well, like I said, the coaches really did a great job of reminding all the pitchers: "Whether you were in the rotation or not, to be prepared to pitch." And when Dick told me, I just remembered something Tom Seaver told me when I met him as a kid.

I was always into baseball, and I went to a million games at the Vet in Philly when I was a kid. That's where I grew up. One day, I met Tom Seaver there. He was one of the first big leaguers I ever met. I saw him and I said, "I gotta talk to him."

I was already developing into a drop and drive pitcher, like Seaver, and I was killing my kneecap. So I asked him about that, and he told me to wear those knee pads like the basketball players wear. The next day, literally, I went out and got a pair of $5 knee pads.

But, the other thing he told me, he said the most important day for any starting pitcher is not the night before the start, it's the night before the night before. That's when you need to get a great night's sleep. And I was scratching my head, thinking that doesn't make any sense… But he explained that the night before you're scheduled to pitch, you're too keyed up to sleep anyway. You'll be playing out the game in your mind. So as long as you get a good night's sleep two nights beforehand, you'll be rested. So when my dad and my uncle and everybody's up there in my hotel room snoring away, I didn't sleep real well but I was still refreshed for Game 6 because I had slept perfectly the night before that.

So just those little nuggets you find out from guys that have been successful really helped me out, and it's something not only I lived by the rest of my career but I even told young pitchers that and those young pitchers, like even here when I talk to Jared Weaver and Garret Richardson and other guys on the Angels, they know that story too. You learn stuff like that and pass it on.

CT: So now it's Game 6, you're a 22-year-old second-year pitcher, and you're pitching against the Toronto Blue Jays, a great team at the time. It's a must-win game. There's probably no other position in baseball where the pressure is greater than on a pitcher in the postseason, particularly a starting pitcher. If things don't go well, it's on you. How did you focus all of that stress and manage all of that going into that start and during the start?

MG: I know it sounds odd when I say this but it felt really good to be in a position to determine whether we were going home or advancing to Game 7. I mean, going back to my time growing up, playing with my friends in the schoolyard in Philly, I wanted to be that guy. I loved pitching big games. And when I was left out of the rotation, initially, I was worried I wouldn't get that chance. And, well, I got it [laughs].

You know, there's that ongoing debate around baseball every time a pitcher wins the MVP Award, like [Clayton] Kershaw did [in 2014]: "How can he win the MVP? He doesn't play every day." A pitcher may only pitch every four or five days, but when he's out there he has more of an impact whether his team wins or loses than any other player. A position player might hit .333, but he can do that by going three-for-four one day, and helping his team win, and by going oh-for-four the next day and not being a factor. If a pitcher has a bad day, chances are the team loses. So guys like Kershaw, when they are so dominant, deserve consideration for the MVP—especially if they do it in the postseason.

I've always felt that way about pitching and, when I played, I wanted to be that guy. I always felt like I would succeed and, if it didn't work out, it wasn't because I wasn't prepared mentally or physically. The other guys were just better that day. I was going to make sure that I gave my teammates an opportunity to win. And most times I always felt pretty comfortable regardless of the outcome that I gave my team the chance to win every time I went out there, and I felt that way going into Game 6.

CT: You mentioned Brett offered you words of encouragement. Who were some of the leaders on that 1985 Royals team and how much of a role did they play in the team's success?

MG: We knew going into that American League Championship Series that Toronto was the more talented team, there was no question, just like the [St. Louis] Cardinals were the more talented team in the World Series that year. But, you know, we felt because of the team we had, the guys we had, that they weren't beating us, no matter what. Nobody had come back from being down three games to one in back-to-back postseason series ever before in baseball, yet we did that and we never felt that we weren't going to do that. That was a testament to guys like George [Brett] and Hal McRae and Dick Howser, our manager, because they never had a panicked look on their faces

With all the young pitchers, our entire staff at that point was young, with very little experience. Bud [Black] and Charlie [Liebrandt] had the most experience and they were 26, 27 years old… So we were basically all just kids. But we all fed off the veteran guys we were around because they just knew we were going to do well and that if we all did our jobs[as pitchers], they would be able to do enough to help us win.

CT: Is that mentality the difference between having a successful Major League career and not having one? Is it more than just having a good fastball, or good mechanics, but also the right mentality?

MG: Yes, there's no doubt. I think whether you're a pitcher or even a hitter or any kind of an athlete, if you think you're not going to succeed, then you won't. I even talked to [Oakland A's reliever] Dennis Eckersley about that, during one of our All-Star Games together. I asked him, "How are you so successful?" and he said it was the fear of failure. And that kind of struck me as odd because he looked so extremely confident every time he had the baseball that I would never think he ever feared anybody, but his fear of failure was his driving force.

My driving force and our team's driving force in 1985 was not the fear of failure… It was that we just all as a collective wanted to be that guy, the guy out there with the game on the line. When you feel that you're going to be successful, I think you've got a great chance.

I remember I had one pitching coach that would come out to the mound and say, "What are you thinking of? Why do you keep throwing pitches at a strike zone? You're not focused. You're not this, you're not that…" And lo and behold my next pitch was probably going to be a ball because it didn't do me any good to have somebody come out in an already negative scenario and give me a negative thought. I knew it wasn't going to be good.

So then I had another pitching coach who'd say, "Hey man, you're going to win 20 games. There's no doubt in my mind. Just go out there and relax." Sure enough, I had great success working with him.

Another thing that same coach told me, and I've passed this on to young pitchers I talk to as well, was, "Don't try too hard. Try easy." It's tough to explain that because most everyone thinks that going full bore, giving everything you have, that old cliché of 110%... that all comes into play and that's all fine but you also don't want to put yourself in a position where you're raring back and trying to throw as hard as you can every single pitch.

It's more important to have a game plan, to throw the same way in the first inning as you do in the ninth inning with the game on the line and vice versa. One pitch isn't going to beat you. You need to be consistent and have a consistent approach throughout a game.

CT: Again, you mentioned Brett and McRae as being two key leaders on that 1985 team. Was it stuff they said, like your pitching coach, or something they did that made them effective leaders?

MG: With George and Hal, they weren't necessarily vocal leaders, they weren't coming in there and slamming things, breaking bats, slamming their helmets down, tossing tables in the clubhouse. It was the way they went about their business and the demeanor they had.

Hal was notorious for being one of the best ever at sliding into second and breaking up double plays. I mean, they put a rule in place because of what he used to do to [New York Yankees' second baseman] Willie Randolph. He played the game hard, but never dirty. He played the game, as the old cliché goes, the right way, and we all fed off that.

I've always been a big believer in body language, in the idea that how you carry yourself, in whatever it is you do and whatever situation you're facing, is important. I had an uncle who worked in the CIA. He was actually killed in Beirut in 1983. But he was a high-ranking guy in the CIA and nobody around him had any idea. I mean, just the way he carried himself... Tough, strong, but humble.

Now whether that ability to do that makes you successful or not, I don't know, but [George and Hal], with their body language, their facial expressions day in and day out, they were extremely positive all the time. It was amazing.

Me? I'd be dishonest if I said my [body language] was positive all the time because it wasn't. Something would inevitably happen during the course of a game that wasn't positive, and I might react to that. But I always looked at those guys, I'd see them and go, "Yeah, okay, now I feel pretty good."

I remember George came in after we lost Game 4 of the World Series in St. Louis. We're down three games to one, and he literally walked into the clubhouse and said, with a straight face, "Hey guys, we've got them exactly where we want them. We're going to win the next two games just like we did in the last series." And he went and took his cleats off and sat down and did his customary stuff after a baseball game and never said anything else. You're waiting for him to laugh, waiting for him to slam something, but that was it. And then all of a sudden, I feel like we all looked at each other and said, "You know what? He's right. All we need is to get off to an early start or do something successfully, one of us, catch a baseball, make a good pitch, make a good at bat, steal a base, whatever it was, we're going to win this thing."

And lo and behold, we got a break in Game 6 on the call at first base and we win that game even though I always point out to all the Cardinals fans, there was still only one out when we scored that run so it doesn't mean we weren't going to score... even if there were two outs and Jorge Orta was called out on that play, there's still a chance we were going to tie or win that game anyhow... We still had another at bat and the way we were playing, there's no way we weren't going to score.

CT: Now you grow into obviously being one of the leaders of the Royals staff as your career goes on, and you were there unfortunately for the beginning of the time when the Royals weren't as successful. Was it challenging for you and your teammates to keep a positive outlook during years that weren't as successful?

MG: It was tough because as my career started to progress and I became more successful, more and more guys that were entwined in those winning ballclubs [with Kansas City], both the playoffs and into the World Series, were all eventually moving on and I think after 1993 when George [Brett] retired, I might have been the only one still left that even had any kind of feel or connection with that successful [1985] club.

And then all of a sudden you're the leader, you try to tap into the successful years the franchise had. Myself and Jeff Montgomery, who had a very successful career closing for the Royals, we would bring together the whole team every single night after every game. If we were home we might go out to dinner or if we were on the road we might gather in somebody's hotel room and have sodas or beers or whatever, we'd have some music, and guys would hang out every night and talk about the game, joke about the game, rib each other about the game but also talk about how we could be better and what we could do to bring back the "Royal Way," and that was winning, and consistently winning.

Clearly it didn't work out for 29 years until [2014], but we felt we were close. In 1994, before the [players' union] strike, we had won 14 games in a row and we were as good as anybody outside of Cleveland in baseball at that point, so we knew we were on the right track… But after the strike, a number of players left the organization so we were all the way back to square one.

CT: I know that you've had some issues in your family with your daughter Ashley having some health issues. How did you manage that crisis in your personal life?

MG: Yeah, that was really a difficult time. Ashley was four years old and she's in preschool when she started having seizures. My daughter Nicolette and my son Chad were so-called normal healthy kids, so we were kind of caught off guard. We couldn't figure out what was wrong with her initially, and then she started complaining about her stomach and then we'd see her just staring blankly at you and sort of blinking her eyes and kind of doing things with her hands....

So finally we saw a neurologist after seeing her doctor and next thing we know, she's diagnosed with seizure disorder. And, at that point, we were relatively young parents and Ashley's having seizures daily, sometimes a number of times a day, but each day the doctor kept telling us, "Send her to school, do this, do everything normal, play soccer..." We're trying all sorts of medications, treatments, whatever and nothing's working. She would have seizures and stuff on the soccer field, playing baseball, did the same thing in school and we kept trying different medications. And that was extremely difficult. You're trying to think in terms of telling the two older kids that their sister's going to be fine. We'd keep telling each other, my wife and I, that she's going to be fine. And we kept grasping at things that are positive, like the doctor telling us there's a good chance she'll outgrow it. Still no medication's working.

And then finally she has a major grand mal seizure at school and the helicopter lands in the school yard and she's non-responsive. They had to airlift her to the hospital. My wife goes in the helicopter and I'm following the helicopter down to UCLA. We were trying to get to UCLA for awhile but it's very difficult because I guess the list of people trying to get in there from all around the world, to get in there to see the doctors there.

Eventually, we did MRIs, none of them showed anything, and then finally the radiologist there did a PET scan, an MRI and a CAT scan. She fused them all together and points to the spot exactly where it's causing these seizures, and we're like, "Okay, so what do we do?" That's when we met with a surgeon, who told us they would have to surgically remove part of her brain. When you hear that news as a parent, you're thinking, "Oh man..."

But I loved this surgeon. I mean, he was extremely up front about everything, all the risks and everything behind it and he said, "Do you want her to have her best opportunity to be the kid she wants to be or do you step back and be protective like parents do and should be and take the risk that not only she'll never be the way she wants to be, that her life could be shortened because of it?" He just exuded confidence...

CT: Exuded confidence how?

MG: He was straightforward and a lot of times as a parent, you want the doctor to just say, "Oh everything's going to be perfect. Oh, she won't feel any pain. There won't even be a scar..." But that's not always reality.

He was extremely confident in what he was going to do, in his plan. He was going to do this and this...because he fell in love with our daughter, just like my wife and I. He said, "This kid is going to be special..." And because of him, I was so confident. I'm like, "Boom, I'm good," even though my wife's like still nervous, which you expect and hope from your wife and the mother of your child, that that's the way she was going to be, but as soon as I saw his face there, outside the OR, I knew my daughter was in good hands.

CT: How is she doing now?

MG: So Ashley eventually has surgery on the day before Thanksgiving, six years ago now, and since that point she's been great. She's playing on the high school softball team and doing well in school. It was difficult for her. She had tutor after tutor. Now she doesn't need a tutor and she's doing well. She's my tough one.

We still battle through some things. She's living as normal a life as possible, but we can't let her play soccer anymore because it's too difficult to run out there on the field and grab her when she's having a seizure.

CT: Is it difficult for you being away from home even now that she seems to have turned the corner?

MG: Oh yeah, you always dread every conversation or every phone call, yeah, no doubt. But she's at the point now where she tells me, "Dad, I'm fine, I'm fine, I'm fine, I'm fine. Let me grow." She always says, and she still crushes me on this every day, "I'm not your little girl anymore. I gotta grow."

And I always think, "Okay, but your roots aren't going far away from me, that's for sure." So it's difficult but we make the effort to stay in touch when I'm on the road and, you know, the lucky thing about my job now is that from October all the way through until April, I'm home every day. By spring, she probably wants me to go back to work.

My wife has been outstanding with it and as a mom. I think it's more difficult for her than anything else. As your mom, it's in your genetics to always worry, so she's always worried.

We do take a lot of heat from her because there's things she can't do that other kids do, sleepovers, things like that. But she knows that, she's aware of it and she's really positive about it.

CT: Good to hear. What's the future hold for you, Mark?

MG: Well, I hope to keep doing the broadcasting work, obviously, and I'm coaching a bit for Chaminade High School out here in Southern California, just when I can. I just help out as much as possible, especially this time of the year it's easier for me, all the way up until the season starts kicking in mid to late February so I can be in uniform all the way up to when our season starts, which is generally anywhere between April 1st and April 6th I think it is [in 2015]. So I'm around as much as I can.

And because of my daughter I'm still extremely involved in the epilepsy program and neurology program at UCLA. We're actually doing a walk as a matter of fact, Team UCLA, for the Epilepsy Foundation at the Rose Bowl. We do that every year. I'm on the board, trying to do as much as possible, because dealing with an illness in a child was the hardest thing I ever dealt with in my whole life.

When my own child was at UCLA, walking through the halls, I almost couldn't make eye contact with other parents because I knew what they were going through and a lot of them were going through a heck of a lot worse things than I was going through. It's hard. It's hard on parents. I love that certain organizations really deal with the fact not only is the child getting all that care but dealing with the whole mental stuff with the parents. It's so stressful, so it's great that the support services are there. And UCLA does such a great job with that. I'm proud to help in any way I can.

Author's note: Those who know "Gooby" as he's called by friends in the baseball fraternity aren't surprised that he's learned from a challenge in his personal life and taken it on as a cause. It's what he did on the mound for the Royals in 1985.

Key Messages from Mark Gubicza

Stay ready. When Mark Gubicza was left out of the postseason starting rotation by Royals manager Dick Howser in 1985, he could have sulked. Instead, he prepared himself to pitch—every day. The approach paid off. When he was called upon to pitch the pivotal Game 6 in the American League Championship Series that year, he threw a gem and helped his team make it to the World Series, which they eventually won. The story illustrates that plans don't always work out. Be prepared for emergencies and have contingencies in place when things don't quite work out like you had them drawn up.

Stay positive. Gubicza's story about the pitching coach who came out to the mound to criticize the pitcher during poor outings speaks volumes about how the demeanor of a leader can have an effect on the team. If your people see you angry or flustered in times of crisis, they will take cues from you. Similarly, if they see you more concerned with finding someone to blame for problems, they will be more focused on that, too.

Chapter Five
Phil McConkey: Super Bowl Champion

He wasn't supposed to even make it to the National Football League (NFL), much less help a team to a Super Bowl championship. Not at 5-10, 170 pounds, and not after taking five years away from the game to fulfill his service obligation after graduating from the United States Naval Academy. But while Phil McConkey wasn't particularly big, or particularly fast—in a sport dominated by players with size and athleticism—he had (and still has) qualities many of his competitors in the NFL, and the rest of us, lack: courage and character.

Those intangibles were more than enough to make McConkey the most reliable wide receiver—and punt returner—on Bill Parcells' New York Giants teams of the 1980s, which brought the franchise and its long-suffering fan base a championship in 1986— its first in three decades. It didn't hurt either that he possessed an intellect strong enough to guide him through Annapolis—and to later lead him to success in the business world as well.

Indeed, McConkey may not have been a star on those teams—what with the likes of Lawrence Taylor, Harry Carson, Phil Simms and Mark Bavaro basking in the limelight. But he always seemed to be around the ball when it mattered most—his touchdown catch early in the fourth quarter of Super Bowl XXI effectively clinched the game for the Giants—and his gutsy, blue-collar playing style forever endeared him to fans of Big Blue.

After a six-year career in the NFL, McConkey could have moved into coaching, but his head and heart led him elsewhere. He ran for Congress in 1990, losing a close party primary to a veteran politician, and immediately thereafter entered the business world, building a career in the financial services industry that has spanned more than two decades (he also had a brief foray into NFL broadcasting, during he won two Emmy awards). With expertise in asset management, trading, alternative investment strategies and investment banking, McConkey has worked for Wells Fargo Bank, Deutsche Bank, BNP Paribas and G.G.E.T, LLC, among others. He now serves as president of Academy Services, a veteran-owned and staffed financial services firm specializing in investment banking, equity markets, public finance and institutional trading. His experiences in the Navy, on the gridiron and on Wall Street have taught him a thing or two about crisis management. Crunch Time caught up with McConkey, who now lives in San Diego, while he was traveling for business—and preparing to pitch Academy Services, and its unique principles, to potential new clients.

Crunch Time: Can you talk about how much you tap into your service experience in your day-to-day work?

Phil McConkey: We're an institutional broker dealer, so we do municipal bond underwriting, corporate underwriting, equity and debt, and we do trading of fixed income equity securities and investment banking, those kinds of things.

Our goal here is to bring military veterans alongside financial services veterans, by taking the experiences and the skills that each of those two entities possess. And we've found and our clients have found that it's not just an additive, it's a multiplier. So we try to have a 50-50 split because the industry veteran can teach the military veteran about financial services and then, more importantly or equally as important, the military veteran comes in with their unique skill set.

Now what do I mean by that? What we're trying to do is take the best of the military culture and bring it to our customers in financial services. And when I talk about the best of the military culture, and it sounds very cliché to throw these words around but it really resonates and it's true, things like honesty, integrity, loyalty, teamwork and oh, by the way, something called service. We are in a service industry and that's too often forgotten. Yet for the military part of our business, service is number one in the lives of these people.

Now let me tell you the difference. I joined the military in 1975. A war had ended a year and a half before, Vietnam. All these people that we've hired and we've brought into our company, all the military people out there that are transitioning back to civilian life that are still active, the majority of them, the great majority of them, think about this, they joined the military after we were attacked on 9/11, after the war in Afghanistan started, after the war in Iraq started. So when you're talking about crises, crisis of individual, of team, of unit, of life, I mean these people have been through it.

CT: So your point is, that you're not just helping

Now I was in a cold war but I didn't have anybody shooting live bullets at me, I didn't have to avoid an IED. I'm looking at a new hire, a young man in the Marine Corps whose vehicle was blown up by an IED. The fact that he survived is miraculous and he's sitting there in a wheelchair, paralyzed from the waist down, no use of his triceps, can barely use his hands, and he's sitting there and says, "I don't want to be known as the guy in the wheelchair, I want to be known as the best salesman you've got…"

CT: So your point is, that you're not just helping that young veteran out, giving him a new job. That young man's commitment and understanding of service will help your firm and your firm's clients in the end?

PM: Right.

CT: There's been a lot of talk about how we treat veterans in this country. And here your firm is one of those that are trying to change some of the bad statistics we've read about in terms of high unemployment among recent veterans. How do you think we're doing in this regard?

PM: It's a hell of a lot better than what it was. Oh my God, it's night and day the way our country, our people, our companies are treating military veterans that are coming back. In 1975, I was an 18-year-old kid from Buffalo. I didn't know crap and I was being spat upon, called a warmonger, right? Now people thank you for your service. There's Veterans on Wall Street, J.P. Morgan, our partner who invested in us, started the "100,000 Jobs Mission," they've now hired 200,000 veterans into Wall Street firms. There are 1,500 corporations that have included veterans in their supplier diversity program. The outreach is phenomenal. I'm coming back to New York in two weeks, for the Veterans on Wall Street affair. I'm so proud of our country for what we're doing for our veterans.

CT: But there is still more work to be done, don't you think?

PM: Absolutely. Until every one of these people gets a job, absolutely. And there's a lot of them that don't, and that's part of what our mission is at Academy Services. And see, here's the thing. Wages are rising in our country, especially in the tech sector. The reason is we're not training enough people to be qualified in those skills to get jobs; we're just not. And so what happens? There's a demand, the supply is low, wages go up.

The transitioning military veteran today—two million of them have transitioned or are transitioning with another million behind that, and it's not going to go away because war and conflict is not going to go away—for these people, everything they do in the military is surrounded by technology. You drive a tank. You operate a weapon. It's all about technology. They have the requisite skill set to fill those technology-oriented jobs where there's a demand. It's matching the two. It's getting the veteran to understand, and we do this every day, we're a for-profit business and we're out there doing underwritings and banking deals and all that but our social mission is to help veterans get jobs, we counsel and mentor and tutor and help network for these people all day long. The big thing is getting them to understand about all their skills and their experiences and how well they translate back to the private sector. They've got to have that confidence because some of them just flounder and are not sure what they can do or what they're capable of and then it's getting the company side, the private side, to understand how those skills can fill a huge void in their company.

As a former NFL guy, semi-celebrity, I've been paid I can't tell you how much money to go to corporations and talk to their executives, to their people, about leadership and teamwork. Who embodies those qualities better than a military veteran? I go to these companies all the time and say, "Heck with it. Save your money on that. Hire these great people and change the culture of your company from within instead of putting a Band-Aid on it, giving money to people that don't need it."

CT: Your point is that anybody who enters the service academies, they're making a commitment. They're not committing themselves just for four years of education. They're committing themselves for five years beyond that, which you obviously know from personal experience. Can someone who doesn't have a military background build the same knowledge and experience?

PM: You can't because when you sign up for the military, it's about the team, it's about your unit, it's about your Army, your Air Force, your Navy, your Marines, that's first, right? And you go to Wharton and you're getting your MBA to go get an investment-banking job on Wall Street and it's about you. And where's the commitment? I mean are you committing to a company for five years after school? I don't think so. If somebody gave you a better deal, you're jumping ship. So the mentality of the military veteran is completely different, and I'm not saying it's better and I'm not saying it's universal, but there's the head start that you get with a military veteran. They've already committed, they've already served, they've already sacrificed, they know how to work together and they're honest and they have great integrity. Listen, again there are exceptions but I'm talking in general terms. That's what you're getting.

Look, by my nature, I have a positive outlook. There's no way I couldn't at one hundred sixty pounds barely, twenty-seven years old, [having not played] football five years. I wouldn't have come close to making it to the NFL without that as part of my make up. Growing up, in the 1960s, I remember going under the desk in school because we were going to get nuked by the Soviets. The way I grew up, we thought we were middle class. Today we'd be on food stamps. We'd be labeled poor. All you hear about in the media today is the problems, the lack of leadership, oh woe is us...

STOP! Look at the people that are coming back to our country and transitioning. They joined the military after all these things happened to us, and they've got character and honesty that's through the roof. They're the ones that are going to be leading us. We're in really good hands. I've got friends who are worth more than we could ever imagine, who live in the lap of luxury and their offspring, their sons, their daughters are going to war, joining, volunteering. Nobody's drafting them. I can name you two dozen right off the top of my head that I know firsthand. Captains of industry, their sons and daughters are joining. We're in good hands with these people.

And not only are we in good hands I think politically but business wise as well. Like there's no difference, and I'm telling you there's no difference at all, between the Greatest Generation and these people that I've just spoken about. The Greatest Generation saved us from tyranny, saved the world from tyranny, in World War II and came back and built us to levels of prosperity unseen in the history of the civilized world, right? This is the next Greatest Generation right now. We're in the middle of it. We don't see it all the time but we are. And I can't wait till these people start running for office and become politicians and taking over businesses and companies.

CT: Should we bring back the draft or have mandatory military service, so that more people get an education in service and commitment?

PM: I'm kind of conflicted with that. I really am, because on one side of me I think everybody should serve, I think everybody should have that experience because I think it really lays an incredible foundation for you for the rest of your life. I think it's an experience that we all should share.

On the other hand, I'm all about freedom, and if you don't want to do it, that's fine, too. So I kind of go back and forth.

CT: Your response is interesting, and you make a great point. Can you talk about your own service in the Navy?

PM: I graduated from the Naval Academy, I went to flight school, I got my wings as a helicopter pilot. I wanted to be a jet pilot but I didn't have the stomach for it so I flew helicopters. I flew the Boeing H46 and those are those long tandem rotor helicopters. The Army calls them Chinooks; ours were called Sea Knights.

What we did was mostly was called "vertical replenishment." Basically, we'd carry loads externally from ship to ship. We carried nuclear weapons. I was a nuclear weapons trans-shipment pilot, which actually sounds worse than it is because you could drop a nuke from one thousand feet and nothing is going to happen but you could drop a conventional bomb from one thousand feet and chances of detonation are pretty good. So the nukes are actually safer to some degree.

Anyway, I did that and then, this is in the early eighties, we were building up to a 500-ship Navy under Ronald Reagan and we were driving the Soviets to the breaking point, so the Cold War was in high gear and there was espionage under the sea with nukes running around. So I helped support the fleet on a storage ship, making sure the battleships had adequate supplies. Was it dangerous? Yeah. You try to land a helicopter that big on the back of a rolling pitching deck at night when you've got about fifteen feet of clearance between the tips of the rotor blades and the super-structure of the ship. Yeah, it's dangerous. But, nobody was shooting at me and that's a big difference.

I actually feel very uncomfortable when people thank me for my service. I feel uncomfortable because I can't even relate or compare it to the service that these post-9/11 kids have been involved with or even the guys that preceded me, the Vietnam and Korea guys. So yeah I'm proud of it, and I did it, and I wanted to go on to something else but if times were different, I often wonder how I would respond. If we were in a crisis and were in a war at the time, would I have had the courage that all these young people had to stay in the military instead of chasing my dream to play pro football?

CT: Knowing what I know about you, I think you'd probably say "Yes" to that. But, since you brought it up, on to your football career. Obviously it was a very successful one, especially given that you came out of the Navy. What do you think was key to that success, being part of a Super Bowl winner?

PM: Well, there's a lot of ingredients to the secret sauce of being a champion and winning on a consistent basis and I learned it early on. It went through my military career, my professional football career and in my business career right now the way we run our company. In a lot of places, a lot of entities, you've got your superstars, your top people, your big time management, right? They run the company or the team and they're the most important people and the focus is always on them. I learned early on that to be extremely successful, to win, to handle any crisis, every single person on the team has got to be made to feel important. So let me give you a great example.

On my team, the Giants, boy, you knew Lawrence Taylor was important, you knew Phil Simms, he was the quarterback, he was important, and Harry Carson, he was important. Well, the Parcells and Belichicks of the world, and you hear [current Giants head coach and assistant in the 1980s] Tom Coughlin talking about it now, these are all guys I played for, they understand to overcome extreme odds, the fifty-third guy on the roster needs to be made to feel like he's important.

I was a lowly punt returner. That job is the worst job in pro football. In fact they did a survey a few years ago, they asked what's the hardest job in pro football—it's catching punts. Forget about getting hit, no! They're not worried about that. Forget about the danger. It's just catching a punt with the wind and the spin and judging as to where it goes, that is the hardest job. As a punt returner, I was always made to feel like my job, what I did, was as important as anybody else on the team. Now when you foster that kind of spirit, everybody's pulling together and it is truly a team.

Now we had a great example of that when we went into the NFC Championship Game [in 1986] against Washington at our place. Well, there were winds gusting to 50 miles an hour. I caught like six or seven punts, I might not have gained 10 yards, but I caught them. I didn't let them hit the ground and Parcells in his book and he's publicly stated it, he said later, "The guy that won the game was the punt returner because he didn't let any punts hit the ground and it was worth one hundred yards or more field position." We got into a situation where what I did as punt returner could have been the difference from winning and losing that day. Washington's punt returner let them all hit the ground.

The thing that sticks out to me about those teams and those people, those coaches, the success that Coughlin's had... I mean, how many Super Bowl rings between those guys? Parcells, Coughlin, there's four. Belichick's got four. There's eight Super Bowl rings among the coaches I played for, and I think the key to that success is that they make every player on their teams feel important, that the job they do and what they contribute to the team is important. I've tried to have the same philosophy at my company, and it's a lesson I learned in the military, too.

I was flying the aircraft, but the guy that was tightening the bolts on the bottom of the aircraft, he was part of our team, and he was as important as I was if not more. He doesn't do his job and we're all in a lot of trouble. If he doesn't tighten that bolt, I'm dead. The mission fails. If the punt returner fumbles the ball, you lose. My company, our company now, the perceived lowest person on the totem pole is made to feel as important as me, the president, because we're not going to win unless we take care of every bit of data that goes through this company. So that to me is a huge key.

CT: You had a chance to coach after you stopped playing, right?

PM: Right. I could have been on the [Giants'] 1990 [Super Bowl-winning] team as a coach. After the 1989 season, I was done. I was thirty-three years old and ancient by NFL standards. I got out unscathed, which was pretty amazing at my size.

So I knew it was time to get out and Coach Parcells called me and told me that Romeo Crennell was moving over from special teams coach to take over defensive line, because the defensive line coach had retired. Mike Sweatman, who was the assistant special teams coach, was going to be special teams coach so there was an opening for assistant special teams coach.

Parcells calls me into his office, and he said, "Listen, as head coach of this team I need to put together the best staff and have the best people fill every position and as far as assistant special teams coach, as head coach, I'm offering you that job." But, in the next breath, he said, "As your friend, I'm advising you not to take it."

CT: Really? Why did he do that?

PM: Because he knew what I was looking for and he knew my personality, not that I was bored with the X's and O's but I was looking to do something different.

Parcells had to fill that position so he found a high school coach in New Jersey named Charlie Weis. Whenever I see Charlie, I say, "Charlie, if I didn't turn that job down, you'd still be coaching at Immaculata High School" or wherever the hell he was at the time. Charlie may never have gotten that chance again.

[Author's Note: Weis went on to have a successful career as an NFL assistant coach and a head coach at the college level at the University of Notre Dame and the University of Kansas.]

CT: Parcells, though, knew you were interested in going into the business world, I assume. A lot of professional athletes have a tough time making that transition.

PM: Right. They struggle.

I talk to my daughter about this, my 11-year-old, and I talk about this with young people all the time in my public speaking work. Life is a series of events where you start at the bottom and struggle to get to the top and then turn around and you're right at the bottom again. And for me it started in grammar school. You get to 8th grade and you're at the top and then you go to high school, and you're at the bottom again.

I get to my senior year in high school and I'm at the top, then I go to the Naval Academy and I'm a plebe. I'm the lowest on the totem pole. Eventually, I become a captain on the football team my senior year, and I graduate and enter the Navy and I'm an Ensign, the lowest again, but pretty soon I start to rise up through the ranks.

I get out of the Navy, I go to preseason training camp with the Giants. [Author's Note: Navy coach Steve Belichick arranged the tryout; his son Bill was an assistant coach with the Giants at the time.] Supposedly, I've got no chance of making the team, not at my size, not after five years away from the game competitively. I mean, there's fourteen wide receivers going to camp, they're going to keep four, maybe five. I was the second oldest; there wasn't a guy within twenty pounds of me. And I fought and scratched and clawed and I got to be a part of something really special and win a Super Bowl and score a touchdown in the Super Bowl and realize a dream.

When it was over, when I retired and turned down that coaching job and decided to enter into business, I knew I was going to go back down to the bottom again. I had to learn a new career, right? Even if I'd stayed in coaching, I was going to be assistant special teams coach—I was going to be the low guy on the totem pole. So I was ready for that, but most guys that play in the NFL, or play professional sports, aren't because, if you think about it, they have an extremely special and rare talent that was recognized early on in their lives and because of that rare special talent, they were treated differently. They were special. And by the time they retire, all they know about is being considered special, better than everyone else. If you go through Little League to high school, college, pro football and you're thirty-something years old when you're done, all you've ever known is being told how great you are. Now, you've achieved this high, high level and you expect to stay there because that's where you've been.

And for a lot of people it's tough to come down. It's tough to go back to school and get your insurance licenses. It's tough to go to school again at that age and get your securities licenses, it's tough to start at the bottom to learn a new profession. I was eager to do that, where I think a lot of people have a big problem with that adjustment. It's not the adjustment away from pro football. It's not the adjustment away from the adulation and the cheering and the big money. I think it's just the realization that you've got to start at the bottom again. They're not well equipped for it.

Athletes who play professional sports, they have many of the same qualities that the military veterans have. Everything I just talked about with the military veterans, those great skills and qualities… It may not be the technology side but, man, to play a professional sport, you know the discipline you have to have? Do you know the ability to work and attain goals, the willingness to sacrifice that you have to have? All those qualities translate to the business world. Whether you want to work for a company or start your own company, it's all the same. But you know, getting those people to understand that they have it within them to be wildly successful in the business world, the perseverance, the drive, that's not always easy, especially when you tell them they have to start at the bottom, just like everybody else.

Let me give you a great example. Military veteran, right? I had a guy who came in one day and the first thing we say to them is, "You've got to kind of find out what your own personal situation is. Are you at a stage in your life where you've got to work for a big company and have security like the military, you get your pay check every month, or are you an entrepreneur? Can you go hungry for awhile until you build something up? Are you okay with that?"

And then, whichever one they pick as the next phase of their lives, whether it's working for a big corporation, a company, or being an entrepreneur, it's about finding their talent. Are they a salesperson? Are they somebody that likes to be outside the office or are they a back office person? Are they compliance? Are they bookkeeping? Are they administrative types? Anytime you start a new phase in your life, or enter a new line of work anyway, you've got to ask yourself these types of questions and be able to answer them.

Anyway, we had one kid, and I'll never forget it, he says, "You know? I don't care, entrepreneur, big company. I just want to sell, I want to be out there and sell." And then he asked me, "What's the hardest part of selling?" And I told him, "Well, you've got to be very persistent. You've got to be able to accept no a lot more than you hear a yes."

I told him, in fact, that the hardest thing to do if you think about it is doing a cold call. He asked me, "What's a cold call?" I told him it's when you pick up the phone and you call somebody, you want to sell them something, a product or a service, and you don't know who they are and you've got to introduce yourself; that's a cold call. And I said a lot of times the person you're calling will just hang up on you before you can even get out your name.

And this young man said, "That's the hardest part?" I said, "Yeah, that's it." And do you know what he said? He said, "Man, I'm gonna kick ass in this joint! I was just getting shot at and evading land mines. That's hard. Having somebody hang up on me is not hard at all, and if that's the hardest thing, boy, I'm gonna kick ass." And, you know what? He has.

CT: Great story. Based on your experience, what do you think is important for managers in a time of crisis?

PM: Both in football and in the military, you practice everything. You do tons of drills. It's all about repetition, and sometimes for a player or a service member that repetition gets so boring it's nauseating; you're just sick of doing it.

As a pilot in the Navy, no matter what you're flying, you have a checklist. You have this sort of clipboard attached to your thigh in the cockpit, and there's a checklist of the protocols you have to follow. And it's there so you can read while you're flying. Some of these checklists are twenty, twenty-five items deep, even before you can take off. And you went through these checklists so often, everyday, sometimes multiple times a day, you had them memorized. You didn't need to look at them. But we were trained to look at them at every opportunity throughout a mission because you can never predict what happens. Nobody is perfect, and if you miss one of those items on the checklist in a time of crisis, it could be the difference between life and death. So we had to train ourselves and it was hard because this stuff is so ingrained into your brain, to stick with that checklist to make sure you avoid a crisis.

And then flying, everything we did, all we did was training for a crisis situation. A hydraulic light goes off, well what do you do? Well, you have items that you had to do in order and you had to memorize those because you didn't have time to look at a checklist, right? And you had to do them in order, quickly, or you could crash, burn and die. And that's all you did all day every day when you were flying. It's all about anticipating and preparing for crises. So the crises and the handling of those crises, the important steps don't happen after it happens, it's before it happens. You plan and you drill over and over and over and over. And even then you're not going to be 100%, but at least you're somewhat prepared.

Author's note: That McConkey has been at least "somewhat prepared" for every challenge he's tackled in his life would be an understatement. To those who have served with him, played football with him and worked with him, that the "little" wide receiver from Navy continues to achieve success comes as no surprise.

Key Messages from Phil McConkey

Identify team members who are committed to the cause. Anyone who dedicates their life to a cause—be it a military or social one—has shown a tendency to remain committed, even in the face of adversity. Managers need to be able to identify these same qualities within their teams. Who is committed to helping the company out of a crisis? Who is looking to jump ship and find another job when crisis hits? A company of loyal, committed employees will always succeed.

Have a crisis checklist. Even the best-trained, best-drilled Navy pilots, and football players, need to have mental checklists, reminders of what to do in certain situations. That's why Navy sailors perform drills, and that's why athletes practice. Have procedures and protocols in place for every function within your division or organization, so that if someone needs to step in and take on a new task on short notice, they have the information they need to hit the ground running. Update these procedures as needed, and train and re-train staff until they become rote.

Make everyone on your team feel important. McConkey is being modest when he says he played the least important position— punt returner—on those Super Bowl-winning Giants teams, but his point about making everyone on the team or within the company feel important still rings true. If crisis hits, everyone will need to pull together. In some cases, all employees in the organization, those at the top as well as those at the bottom, will need to make sacrifices. They may need to work extra hours or take pay cuts. Getting this type of loyalty and esprit de corps from staff is as easy as making them feel part of the team every day, in each and every thing you do as their manager. Sounds cliché, but it's true.

Chapter Six
Jackie Joyner-Kersee: Track & Field Olympic Gold Medal Winner and World Champion

The sport of track and field has arguably been facing a crisis for some time now. Despite the fact that some of the world's finest athletes can be found among distance runners, sprinters and long jumpers, etc., track and field receives all too little attention in non-Olympic years—and, recently, much of the attention it has received has been for all the wrong reasons.

Namely: cheating.

As in baseball, American football and cycling, the use of performance-enhancing drugs (PEDs) by a number of track and field stars has led to a hue and cry from the sports press and fans alike, and calls for more stringent testing protocols and stricter punishments for those caught using PEDs. Some of the biggest names in the sport—Canada's Ben Johnson and Marion Jones and Tyson Gay of the U.S.—have been implicated in doping-related scandals, and several others have been hounded by persistent accusations.

One of the sport's modern legends, Jackie Joyner-Kersee, has taken a brave stance on the issue of doping, calling for those caught to be banned from the sport and its biggest competitions—including, obviously, the Olympics—for life. She has described the issue of PEDs in track and field as "an arms race" that has "hurt the sport" deeply.

After a stellar career during which she won six Olympic medals (Silver in heptathlon during the 1984 Olympic in Los Angeles; two Golds in the heptathlon and long jump in 1988 in Seoul, South Korea; Gold and Bronze, respectively, in the same two events during the 1992 Games in Barcelona; and Bronze in the 1996 Olympics in long jump in Atlanta) and multiple medals in the sport's World Championships, among other accolades, Joyner-Kersee has served on the board of USA Track and Field (USATF) since 2000, and been actively involved in promoting the sport and working with young people.

Although she faced doping allegations herself late in her career—in spite of having never tested positive for PEDs—in 2003, she was on the USATF board that voted to institute a lifetime ban for those found guilty of cheating. She also serves as an ambassador with the sport's international governing body, the International Association of Athletics Federations.

Still married to her long-time coach Bob Kersee, to this day, Joyner-Kersee remains a vocal activist on this as well as many larger social issues. In 1988, she established the Jackie Joyner-Kersee Foundation, which provides youth, adults and families with athletic lessons and the resources to improve their quality of life with special attention directed to East St. Louis, Ill. (Joyner-Kersee's hometown).

In 2007, she and fellow superstars Andre Agassi, Muhammad Ali, Mia Hamm, Jeff Gordon, Tony Hawk, Cal Ripken, Jr. and Mario Lemieux, among others, founded Athletes for Hope, a charitable organization that helps professional athletes get involved in charitable causes and inspires millions of non-athletes to volunteer and support charitable causes in their local communities. **Crunch Time** spoke with her as she was traveling back to East St. Louis on one of her many projects.

Crunch Time: Track and Field is obviously a great sport but it's one that doesn't get a lot of attention on the sports radar unless there is a big event, like the Olympics. Is that something that the USATF is trying to address?

Jackie Joyner-Kersee: With our new CEO Max Siegel we're really working on bringing more events to arenas across the country and trying to host bigger events, like the Worlds, here in the U.S. You can see on the collegiate level that there is an interest there but it's just about getting the sport more attention, more coverage, and getting more buy-in from fans. I'm not really sure what makes people gravitate to our sport during the Olympics so I'm not sure how you carry that on outside the Games.

I think some of the things that they're doing with track and field now, hopefully, within the next five years, you will see a change. You're going to see more events being held on the street, in cities across the U.S., for example. But part of the thing I think is that every sport draws interest when there are big-time rivalries between two athletes or two countries. And we don't have that right now, so it would be good to get that built up. It would be great if a U.S. sprinter could challenge Usain Bolt or whatever.

CT: I wonder if some of it has a lot to do with the fact that the sport doesn't have the same sort of personalities like when you were running on a regular basis, granted not that long ago, but still there's no one who sort of seems to have carried on that role. Is that something you agree with or do you think there's people out there we just don't know about?

JJK: I think the rivalries are there. I just think we as a sport need to promote that side of it more. It's really tough to find a niche when you're in the U.S., in a country where so many professional sports are so dominant, but I do feel that we do have a niche here and it's just really up to USATF to carve out that niche. And it might take a longer time to build it but we just need to continue to build from the strengths we have as a sport.

We do have a lot of great personalities but then also a lot of times those personalities are not highlighted until the Olympic year, and then plus it's one thing to have us on television but being on television at a time that's conducive for everybody to watch. You're always going to have those diehard track and field fans. Now, we're really trying to get that crossover, those people that like the sport but don't follow it closely. We're trying to convince them to love the sport and then loving it, maybe following it more regularly. It will help that we're going to have more events around the country where people can see the great athletes we have in the sport.

CT: You've been very vocal about the issue of PEDs over the years. Do you think doping is still a crisis facing track and field?

JJK: Well, I mean it's unfortunate it's out there but we can't continue to live in the past. Not every generation should have to suffer from maybe some things that happened in the past. So I think that you have to move forward and hope that corporations and everyone is going to buy in to the sport and support the younger athletes coming up, and I think they do. They do buy in now, now that they've seen an effort to clean up the sport. I mean, there are just going to be some that think they can take the easy way out, but it's continuing to build the brand because I think the brand is a very strong brand and it's just a matter of us connecting with people that want to connect with our brand.

CT: What do you think was the key to your success as an athlete?

JJK: I would say besides great coaching and training hard, for me I always wanted to be consistent and consistent to me was always being in the mix. I might not have won them all, but I was right there and I tried to figure out what it was going to take for me to go over the top or to get a notch above. So the consistency of competing and trying to stay healthy, and in the sport of track and field, that is really tough because injuries are part of the sport, especially as you get older. So you think you're training right and you're doing everything right and for whatever reason that hamstring just decides, "Okay, I don't want to go today."

CT: Coming from East St. Louis, fairly humble beginnings, was it a challenge for you to get access to the best training and the best coaching? How did you overcome those challenges?

JJK: When I was younger, we really thought we had the best facilities if we weren't running on a dirt track [laughs]. And when you're young, you do whatever your coaches tell you. You believe in them, and you do what they ask of you. And growing up I was in an environment where most of my competitors were facing the same things. It wasn't until I went outside my area, or up another level, that I realized that there was better stuff out there. I would always say every track was bigger than the one I trained on but it wasn't because really all tracks are the same. It's just that some schools had better resources and better facilities.

But as I got better and started getting noticed, I was fortunate to have people sort of take me under their wings and help me get to a better place. When you're in that situation, you need some luck, but you also need to be fortunate to meet the right people. I was fortunate in that way and now that I'm at this point in my life I'm trying to help others get those same opportunities.

CT: You mentioned that when you were competing, that your goal was to try to remain consistent. Looking over your career, you didn't seem to have many low points. Do you remember any low points at all?

JJK: Even though I might have performed well in certain events in the eyes of people outside of my inner circle I guess, there were some that I felt, that I knew that I could have done better. And that was the challenge. As an athlete, you always want to be coachable and not let the news clippings go to your head.

I truly believe in hard work. Whether I won my last race or not, I was always willing to learn more to do well in the next one, to become a better athlete. I learned whatever I could from the people around me, my coaches. I was one that was never satisfied. Yes, I wanted to win, but I also wanted to learn why I wasn't able to succeed in this race or why I wasn't able to execute a jump that I was really prepared to do. Was it something that I was doing or did I go into this race thinking too much or was I too relaxed? Does having the jitters before an event help me or hurt me? Do I need to have the butterflies? Will they help me to focus better?

All those different things that I would try to figure out, how I could become one of the best. And dealing with the ups and downs, and I guess for me the low point probably will always be getting injured. Everyone would always say, "Think positive." But it's hard when you're injured. It's learning how to do that, that is the training that was the most important for me. Not letting that low moment, when you might think your career is over, take over. That's why they have physical therapists, that's why you have a trainer, that's why you have different people, to get you ready and get you back where you should be.

CT: So it's about consulting the experts in those situations I guess then too?

JJK: Right. Because we always train from preventative and really try to prevent anything from happening but sometimes you can do everything right and something still goes wrong. But that doesn't mean that you give up. And that's when it tests you as an individual, because everything seems to come to light when things are not going well. I would always learn from when things weren't going well. All of a sudden the coach was the best coach a week ago, when you get injured, now he's the worst coach. You can't change your attitude like that.

CT: Why do you think you were able to have such a long career? You raced very successfully well into your thirties and almost made it to the 2000 Olympic team. How were you able to do that?

JJK: I think it was the consistent approach and then also being very patient because I was a multi-eventer and that's a blessing in disguise. Being a multi-eventer, I could run the one hundred-meter hurdles well and I could long jump, and I was invited to come to Europe a lot but I would have to sacrifice those meets to train on the events that I didn't care a lot for, like javelin and the eight hundred meters. But I think for my career, a lot of my training was just based around making sure that I was ready to go as a heptathlete, not just as a jumper or a sprinter or whatever. By not going to meets every weekend over in Europe, I was able to keep myself healthy because I was training for the multi-event.

CT: Does it make sense, then, for younger athletes to try and train in multiple sports as opposed to getting into a specialty too soon?

JJK: The basis of any sport is running, jumping and throwing. You might not be the best in all three of the disciplines but you could learn something from training in each of them. When I was coming up, we were just thrown into the multi-event. We didn't know how to do it. I didn't even know how to high jump [laughs]. They just put us into these events. And you find yourself liking it.

So my advice would be to tell people that first of all, you've got to love it, enjoy what you're doing. I think it's great to experiment and to figure out what it is that you want to do. Everybody wants to be that one hundred-meter runner, you know, the fastest person in the world. And that's fine, but I think if you have the ability, a multi-talent or multi-skill, I believe in let's see where that can take you because my attitude was always I can focus on individual events any time I want to.

CT: I asked you what kind of advice you'd give to young track people. Was there anybody we should mention that gave you a lot of advice along the way in your career?

JJK: Oh yeah, I always go back to Nino Fennoy, my coach in East St. Louis. He always believed in progression, and what I mean by progression is that when I was a sophomore, I would make nationals and he would say, "No, you're going to wait till your senior year." Sometimes as young people we taste success so early that then we lose sight of why we're at that position. We don't want to work as hard because now we're entitled, we think it's our birthright that we should go. Nino was about protecting us from that, making sure that we progressed at the right pace, that when we had success we were ready for it.

And, of course, my husband was always my coach. His philosophy was that those who know why can always beat those who know how. A lot of times he would teach all of us, he'd say, "I'm teaching you why you should be doing this because there might be a time where I can't get to the meet, that you'll need to know why you need to be in the warm up two hours beforehand." All those little things played a major role.

And my hero was Wilma Rudolf. She faced so many challenges in her life and in her career, and when I was coming up women's athletics was just getting to the forefront and with great attention came greater expectation. She was a great example of how to overcome that outside stuff, and the pressure she faced was greater than anything I ever faced.

CT: And I guess Athletes for Hope is about finding a Wilma Rudolph or a Nino Fennoy for younger athletes today...

JJK: All of us athletes involved with that sort of knew each other from doing different things, award shows, talk shows, speaking, things like that, even though we all came from different backgrounds and were doing much different things. It started with Andre Agassi and just went from there. And I've become close with Warrick Dunn and Mia Hamm, so it's really been a lot of fun.

So now you might have a collegiate athlete who has a passion for something, who wants to do something in the community, but they may not know where or how to start. So we sort of help them set things up and get them started.

CT: And you're busy with your foundation as well...

JJK: Yeah, I am. We have an annual gala in the fall to raise money for our educational and outreach programs. And I have also been really active on an urban farming initiative in the St. Louis area, educating people on the benefits of urban farming and letting young people know there's opportunities in that space. We have an urban farm in the North St. Louis area with fifty-two acres. We grow sweet corn, radish and soybeans. That's keeping me busy and it's challenging but it's fun and it's something that sort of checks off all sorts of boxes about the needs in an urban community.

I'm into health and wellness and doing different programs in elementary schools with young people, getting them eat a healthy diet, to be active. With physical education programs getting cut in so many schools, kids just aren't learning about healthy living. So what I'm doing now is about filling some of those gaps.

CT: Do you have any advice for managers in a time of crisis?

JJK: A lot of times somehow we don't step back and take a breather before we move forward, because when we're in the crisis, we think, "Everything is crumbling. I can't take a break." But sometimes it's good to step away. In athletics, it's really hard to take a real time out, to get out of the moment. But I always tried to take that time, to count to ten, to take a deep breath, and when I did that I could feel myself starting to relax and then I would be able to take on the next challenge.

Key Messages from Jackie Joyner-Kersee

Teach the why, not just the how. Great advice from Jackie's husband and coach, Bob Kersee. Often managers have difficulty delegating, particularly in times of crisis, because they believe they are the only ones who can handle the task. But being a good manager means being a good teacher and empowering your team to take on the challenges and perform the necessary tasks to resolve the crisis at hand.

Take a deep breath. As Jackie admits, this is easier said than done. But while it's important to be proactive, it is also important to make the right decisions and take the *right* actions. And more often than not, that takes time. So even when crisis hits, take a time out and give your mind a chance to evaluate the situation.

Make progress at your own pace. More great advice from Jackie's high school track coach. Our competitive nature often drives us to press ahead, to do better than those we see as adversaries, both within the organizations in which we work as well as in the external marketplace. But while competition is healthy, it's also important to remember that no one wins if you take on a challenge you are unprepared for and fail. Take time to learn and advance when you are ready. It may take a bit longer, but you'll likely find that the success you achieve will endure.

Crunch Time

Chapter Seven
Mike Richter: Stanley Cup Champion

In 1994, goaltender Mike Richter backstopped the New York Rangers to the club's first Stanley Cup in 54 years.

As important as that is for long-suffering Rangers fans (this author included), the club legend, whose name and number hang from the rafters at Madison Square Garden, the American hockey legend hopes he is still writing what will ultimately be his legacy—while making the biggest save of his career: preserving the earth's environment.

After 14-year career in the National Hockey League—all with the Rangers (the quote "Once a Ranger, Always a Ranger" has been attached to his name by the club)—Richter founded Healthy Planet Partners in 2011. The firm combines financial expertise and energy resources to help its client partners operate more efficiently (and, by extension, profitably) while incorporating energy solutions and operating platforms that are environmentally friendly. Indeed, when it comes to crisis management, Richter sees no bigger crisis than climate change, and laments that the issue has become so politicized in the U.S. After all, he says, who doesn't want a cleaner environment?

The goaltender's "new" career should come as no surprise to anyone who followed his old one. Always an intelligent and engaging interview, Richter finished the undergraduate degree he started while playing hockey at the University of Wisconsin at Yale University, after he was forced to retire from hockey in 2003 after sustaining multiple concussions (he says he his healthy now after struggling with post-concussion symptoms for years and has been participating in on-ice Rangers charity events). His degree is in Ethics, Politics and Economics, a knowledge base that certainly serves him well at Healthy Planet Partners.

A three-time NHL all-star, Richter was inducted in the U.S. Hockey Hall of Fame in 2008. As an international, he represented his country in multiple World Junior Championships, World Championships and Olympics, helping the U.S. win a silver medal in the latter in 2002. In 1996, he and long-time Rangers and U.S. teammate Brian Leetch led their national team to triumph in the 1996 World Cup of Hockey, over heavily favored Canada and Russia.

Now, though, Richter's focus (described by Leetch as second to none) is on growing Healthy Planet Partners and expanding support of its stated mission: "to reduce the cost of operating today's facilities while increasing performance and achieving positive environmental change." His aspirations may also lead him into the political arena, and if his hockey career is any indication, his potential opponents should take heed.

Crunch Time caught up with Richter in the spring of 2015, just as his Rangers were attempting to win their first Stanley Cup since 1994.

Crunch Time: You faced a number of crises during your playing career—not the least of which was the Rangers' Stanley Cup jinx—but, on a personal level, dealing with the concussions that ultimately ended your career was probably the biggest challenge you faced, on so many levels. How is your health now?

Mike Richter: Well thank you for asking. I'm doing very well actually. I think it's a difficult injury in that you never know what one hundred percent health is until you don't have it, and then getting it back is by degrees and that can be over a very, very long period.

At this point, do I feel as well as I did the moment before I first suffered a brain injury? Probably not. But I was thirty-six then and in a hell of a lot better shape. Thirteen years later, I think pretty much I've really regained my health. It's an injury that doesn't have a clear path to recovery nor a straight one and, maybe most importantly, there aren't a lot of metrics to make sure that you know when you've recovered, although they are learning more about that all the time.

You can break a bone and they'll say, "You have 6 weeks until you're going to be better." You blow out a knee, it's six months. You twist an ankle, it'll be three weeks. But, you get any kind of trauma to the brain, whether it's a concussion or something even more serious, it's just a feel. There's always those nagging questions, like, "Did I forget my car keys because I got hit in the head or is that just regular old stuff?" But I feel very good, to answer your questions more directly.

CT: Good to hear. I was at the game when you basically blocked a slap shot with your head and I don't know if that was the first injury or one in a series, but I remember being immediately concerned about your health, given the fact that was around the time concussions started becoming a major issue in sports. As an athlete, because of the fact that there's that uncertainty about the injury and it doesn't have the same metrics, as you put it, as other injuries, was that something that was frustrating for you as someone who was always high conditioned and at the top of their physical health?

MR: Yeah. Extremely frustrating. Everything about your job as an athlete actually from a young age on, you don't have to be a professional, but you're rewarded as you move up the pyramid in athletics for being able to put pain or fear or distractions aside and focus on the matter at hand, which is winning the game. And in every injury, I think that holds to the extent that you know what the parameters are, right? Can I play on this bad knee? Yes, you can get through maybe this game. It's a matter of how much pain you can handle, and after the seasons over, after the championship is won, then I can go have the operation, right?

That's not the case necessarily when you're looking at concussion. Even a small one can have profound effects and so to use that same mentality can be very destructive in the short run or the long run. In fact, I think the most impractical thing you can do as an owner of a team is to push a player to play through pain when, you know, maybe a three-week rest or a five-game rest would have allowed him to come back fine later in the season. If you push him too quickly to come back, you can lose him for his career.

Concussions and post-concussion symptoms are one of the most frustrating injuries because there are often no outward signs. Sometimes you actually feel pretty decent until you start working out. In the really acute phase, you feel particularly horrible without doing anything and you're thinking, "Why? It wasn't even that hard of a hit. I've been hit harder before." There's just so many questions and not enough answers now but really good research is being done by fantastic people, so we are in a pretty exciting time of discovery and understanding for what has become a major issue in sports.

CT: I've always admired how, when you unfortunately realized your playing career was over, and all too early, you remained remarkably busy. Was that intentional—so that you weren't sitting around feeling sorry for yourself—or was it a natural extension of your interests in other things besides playing hockey?

MR: I think more the latter but it was a bit of both. Look, you hope you live a long and healthy life and the perspective you can't have as a player, you try to understand the long view but it's very difficult when everything in your life comes moment to moment. That's how you should focus. That's how you should play. Don't worry about next season. Worry about this season. Don't worry about next game. Worry about this game. Don't worry about the next shot. Focus on the present. And that's how you have success as an athlete.

But life needs some planning and you have to understand that the day that you hang up your skates in my case, there's a lot of living left to do and hopefully a lot of contributions you can give to society and a lot of satisfaction you can gain by trying another profession. I think it's becoming more the norm and actually more demanded of people, both in and out of sports. If you want to have true happiness, you'd better be a little light on your feet because gone are the days that you stay at one place for forty years. You better be able to move and pivot and change directions fairly quickly and that can be very stressful, that can be very difficult, but it's maybe a bit more of a reality of life today than it was for our father's or grandfather's generation.

For me, I think the plan was always to go back to school to finish the undergraduate degree that I left to pursue an athletic career, and then see where it took me. I have a lot of interests, but the odd thing is, when you do what I did, going back to school two or three decades later, you're behind the curve with your peers in many of the things that you're doing. I love science, but I hadn't studied it for two decades. So I was never going to walk into my next career after playing hockey for twenty years and say, "Here I am. Let me solve the problems of the world."

You have to start at a lower level, and for athletes who are used to being at the top of their professions, that's actually quite stressful. You tend to gravitate to what you know and, for me, although I had a lot of interests, I had purposely put most of them aside in order to play hockey professionally. So I look at what I'm doing now as a nice opportunity to pursue some of my other interests.

CT: Right. Obviously you have an interest in environment and climate-related issues. How long have you been interested in the environment? Is that something that dates back to your college days, your pre-playing days, or is it something that you picked up in your travels as a player?

MR: I think pretty much I've been concerned about the environment for as long as I can recall. Lots of people come about it from different places but, look, the environment that we live in is important to all of us. If you grew up in an area that has since diminished in the environmental quality, it's something that you… well, you mourn that loss. I grew up outside of Philadelphia and there were just certain things that clicked in my head as a kid growing up. It just seemed like everything was at our fingertips. There was great woods around, hills to sled down, adventures to be had on trails and everything else. There was a beautiful creek that ran through the local area and it used to be stocked with fish. As I got older, however, it became contaminated.

It's part of… you know, it's easy to shrug your shoulders and say, "It's just part of progress," but it's really not. It's an unfortunate byproduct of poor thinking and poor management and it's a terrible outcome. And so really for a profit for a very short period of time, a public good has a great deal of cost associated with it now, maybe forever, and so you can't just let that happen. I think something strikes you even at a young age that that's fundamentally unfair.

There's just so many aspects of the environment that we take for granted, that we let go, for sake of progress, profit, whatever. It doesn't need to be and I think there's kind of a false label we put on this. There's conservative, there's liberal, but in every walk of life, people want to have good water, clean air, healthy environment for their kids and themselves.

You might go about solving environmental problems in a different way and that's fine, those conversations can happen, but we all probably want pretty much the same thing.

You can think about from the social justice standpoint. You can think about it from just a quality of life standpoint. More and more, I think people in the business world are thinking about it as a strategic concept. Ultimately, the economy, everything is bound to the environment. It's part of our lives whether we like it or not, so it's probably a wise thing to take care of it because it's what supplies our food, what we need to sustain life. It's almost hard to extract yourself from the issues, and I think at some point I think we're all going to stop using the idea of, "Boy, you support the environment, you must be for this or against that." There is no such thing as economics that wouldn't support the environment or people that wouldn't be supportive of it.

CT: Is climate change the biggest crisis the planet is facing now, or that business is facing now?

MR: I think it's right up there. I had that experience with that little creek by my house growing up. And then later, living on the west side of Manhattan and looking out on the beautiful Hudson River, I saw a similar thing happening there. In effect, we all sacrificed something that the public here in New York shared, the river, for the sake of profit or at least industry. The river became polluted with PCBs and that ruined the lives of a lot of fishermen and prevented growth of industry that otherwise would have gone on there in terms of recreation and tourism, not to mention drinking water.

It's an amazing thing. Damage to the environment has large, large repercussions and you can't come to the soapbox, "It's only an issue for certain people." We all need a healthy environment for our economic system to work.

When the climate change came along, the first time I had heard of it many years ago, I thought, "Well, there's so many immediate problems, that's a long-term one." But then the more I learned, I realized this isn't our grandson's issue, this is right now. I just read an article about how the number of dead seals washing ashore on the east coast has increased because they've been forced to change their hunting patterns because of warming water temperatures. As a result, they lead their pups to colder water, which is farther away from shore, and the pups can't survive. We're seeing an awful lot of pretty eerie events take place now and I just think as people become more educated on this issue, it's impossible to ignore it. It's so easy, having lived in the east and New York in particular, to divorce yourself from kind of the reality that there is this thing called an environment out there that we actually are a part of even though you forget to see those changes and everything else when you're kind of day to day putting your head down to concrete.

CT: Talk briefly about what your role with Healthy Planet Partners...

MR: Well, I'm the founder and owner of the company and serve as managing director. We're a very small group but we have great people backing us financially and strategically.

I'm in an interesting position where I have an awful lot to learn about the capital markets and running a small business and the industry in which we're focused, which is financing renewable energy and energy efficiency for commercial facilities.

Unfortunately, there are a lot of myths out there about renewable energy, and our message to those we work with is: These are proven technologies. Yes, it's clean and it's healthy and it's good for the environment, but it is also efficient and cost-effective. We're talking to our client partners about energy-efficient lighting, systems that monitor energy usage. Increasingly, we're working with issues such as battery storage, and here in the New York area, since Hurricane Sandy, about emergency power generation.

People are starting to see that we have this aging infrastructure and the utilities are losing sixty, even eighty, percent of their energy over transmission lines from a distance. We're starting to get a little bit more of an idea of how distributed power generation might be wiser. So there are some practical aspects in the immediate-term, but also in the long-term. Yes, we're starting to lower the carbon footprint of these buildings, but we're also making them more efficient.

You look at how efficient Wall Street is and how efficient American businesses are, but the facilities they are housed in still need a lot of improvement in terms of efficiency, operational efficiency. There's a tendency to say, "Oh, it's just a building." Well it's not. Sometimes, operating costs on facilities are one of the largest line items for a business. If you're a business and you can save twenty percent on those costs, then that can be a huge impact. And we're third-party financers, so we help with the capital investment and the client essentially implements these changes at little or no cost.

CT: This question is very cliché so I apologize, but do you draw on any of your experiences as a player in your role now? Are there lessons that you learned as an athlete that you're putting into play in the business world now?

MR: Yes, for sure. Let me put it this way. As a goaltender in hockey, you have to have a bit of a short memory and a long one. Short in that you need to be able to forget a mistake you made that cost your team a goal and move on and be prepared to stop the next one. If I'm one of 700 players in the world that can play at the NHL level, or you're particularly good at what you do and you've worked your whole life to do it, you expect success right away. But, as I was starting this new life and this new profession, I had to remember that even though you expect to see success immediately, because you're used to it, but it doesn't always happen.

And that's when you have to have a little bit of a longer-term view. Just because I can stop a hockey puck doesn't mean that I can manage a company particularly well or that I know how to work my way around the financial models. You have to have enough humility to say, "Okay, look, just as I figured out how to improve my game in hockey when the game started changing, or how I had to get from one level to the next, I've got to figure out what needs to be done and apply myself in this new role."

And I think both remembering how you got to success in your previous career, while at the same time remembering that you're starting from scratch again, is really important. There are people that have been out there for the same three decades that I was playing hockey that were in this very space, this financial space, whether it's engineers or whatever, they have great job experience and you'd better stop and listen to them because they probably have something worth listening to.

I think other things that do translate are the work ethic and the ability to truly manage yourself under pressure. Translating the mental toughness and the trust that you had in your teammates and all those things takes time but it's there and you have an important foundation for how you go about achieving success. I loved playing sports as a kid and I loved playing as an adult, but there's got to be a bigger challenge than just scoring a goal or blocking a shot as you become an adult, and I think that pursuit of excellence in any form is a really fundamentally important thing.

What you're ultimately trying to do is kind of reach your potential wherever you are. And so you just have to start at sometimes a little bit of a lower rung on the ladder and you work your way up. You have to see what needs to be done. Ask yourself, "What do I need to do to get from where I am right now to where I want to be?," and then find a way to just do that. You have to find ways of translating that grit you may have had in the arena to your office space or whatever else you're doing.

CT: You look at athletes who don't have success transitioning into another field of endeavor after they stop playing and then you look at athletes who do and I think that's the difference. It's the recognition that you're going to have to

start from scratch again and not all athletes are able to handle that starting from scratch again later on in life.

MR: There's a weird kind of line that you've got to be able to walk—being comfortable with failure after a career in professional sports, that demands success and not settling for mediocrity.

As an athlete, you cannot be satisfied with where you are, you have to try to keep improving. The Michael Jordans of the world say, "Alright, I'm a really good player but I need to put on more weight." So he goes to the weight room and he comes back the next year even stronger. [NHL star] Sidney Crosby comes in, wins the Hart Trophy [as the league's top scorer], and then comes back and says, "My shot's not good enough," and he goes to work on it. Tiger Woods overhauled his whole golf swing, an incredibly courageous act really. All the personal stuff aside, the guy had won a Master's [tournament] and then he decided to deconstruct his golf swing because as good as he was playing, he knew he wasn't as good as he could be. He knew that was going to mean that he was going to go backwards for a couple months, and he did. Well, guess what? A few years later he's winning everything again and dominating the PGA Tour even more.

For athletes moving into the business world, you have to keep that level of demand of yourself, but at the same time you have to have the patience to say, "Holy smokes, this is a whole new ball game. There's experts in the field, of which I am not one." Know your limitations. And so it's hard. It's hard to ask questions. It's hard not to have answers all the time. You have to rely on other people who have the experience you don't and that can be incredibly uncomfortable, but it is necessary I think. The same excellence achieved as an athlete can be achieved, I think, if you have enough of an understanding that you're not going to be comfortable all the time. You have to accept that there will be some uncertainty as you transition. I think anyone who faces a career change goes through this, though. You're in effect becoming a student again. You have to be able to apprentice yourself I suppose is a good way of saying it.

CT: What does the future hold for Mike Richter? I know you were kicking around the idea of running for political office. Is that something that's still on the table?

MR: I plan to continue to focus on this renewable space. I think it's crucially important. I love the idea of a capital market just being able to solve some of the environmental problems. It's where they often begin and I think it's kind of fitting that you can solve some of the problems the same way. There are a lot of great people in this space, across history, coming up with innovations, whether it's financial investments or technological inventions that make the world better. We're starting to see the fruits of that. Solar panels are going into public houses and what not. It's incredible. It's pretty much a financial invention that allowed a technological invention to flourish. And I like that.

As for politics, look, I've benefited so much from fans the support of people in and around New York, dating back to my days as a player. I really want to leave a mark and make the world a bit better. I really love where I'm at right now, and what we're doing here at Healthy Planet Partners, but some form of public service may be in my future.

Author's note: Richter made this last statement with more than a hint of modesty, but he'd have my vote if he ever decided to run for office—and not just because I'm a fan of Mike Richter: the Hockey Player. When you have the pleasure of speaking with him, you can't but come away impressed with his intellect, his humility and his passion for the work he's doing.

Key Messages from Mike Richter

Have a "short memory" and a "long memory." As a goaltender in hockey, Mike had to be able to forget mistakes and prepare himself to stop the next shot. In business, he believes, it is equally important to put failures and mistakes behind you, but it is also important to take the "long view." Others in this book have reminded us that decisions managers make in times of crisis can have long-term effects, beyond the crisis period. Part of what Mike does in his new role at Healthy Planet Partners is remind companies that making their operations more efficient, from an energy use perspective, does more than help the environment—it also improves the company's bottom line.

"Apprentice yourself." Mike makes the point that, as a professional athlete transitioning to the business world, he had to be open to learning from others with more experience and asking questions. As a successful athlete, and a leader on the teams he played on, Mike was essentially expected to have, as he put it, "all the answers." Entering the new field of environmental/energy policy after 30 years as a hockey player, though, he couldn't have all the answers. Not all of us transition from careers as championship athletes, but we all face change and the challenges it brings in our careers, and remembering that we can always keep learning is important in order to be successful at navigating through them.

Crunch Time

Chapter Eight
Final Thoughts: From the Winner's Circle

The interview subjects in *Crunch Time* have provided us with a sort of checklist for managers who face crises in their day-to-day work. When crisis hits, consider the following:

The Crisis Management Checklist

Assess the crisis. When Nancy took over as coach of the NBADL's Texas Legends, it wasn't exactly a crisis, but she knew from her past experiences as a woman trying out with the Los Angeles Lakers and as a coach and executive with the Detroit Shock in the WNBA—where her tenure didn't end well—that there would be issues for her as a woman coaching men. Rather than pretend these issues didn't exist, Nancy considered them and took them head-on. In the end, her proactiveness served her well, and positioned her to take what she hopes will be the next step— working in the NBA.

"You can't control your reputation, but you can control your

character." This may have been the best comment from Nancy. Managers cannot worry about what others around them think. They have to act, and do so in a way that reflects their values and character.

Draw from past experiences. As Nancy continues to pioneer new trails as first a coach and then an executive in a men's professional sports league, she is able to use her experiences with the Los Angeles Lakers and legendary coach Pat Riley to find common ground with the players in her charge. As the old saying goes, "Experience is a hard teacher," but life's difficulties are meaningless if we don't learn from them. Nancy's outlook on her time with the Detroit Shock is a prime example of that.

Find a mentor. Nancy's friendship with Dick Schaap proved invaluable as she navigated the waters as the face of her sport at only 18 years of age. As Nancy tells it, Dick provided her with guidance in terms of how to act as a professional—and on what to say and how to say it. All leaders and managers need a mentor in times of crisis, someone to serve as a sounding board for ideas, for insights into how to handle personnel matters or address workplace issues. It can be a supervisor or a colleague at a similar level, either within or outside the organization, and the relationship can be a two-way street. But it is vital.

Don't fear your competition. Learn from them. U.S.-Russian relations were hardly warm in the 1970s and 1980s, when Lou Vairo and Anatoli Tarasov became close friends. In fact, as Lou notes, he took some heat from his colleagues at USA Hockey for the relationship. However, hockey was common ground, and the two men learned a lot from one another. Tarasov's approach served as one of the building blocks for USA Hockey's National Team Development Program (NTDP). Established in 1996, the NTDP has trained and developed players in their teens and graduated numerous top performers. It has placed the U.S. national team program on equal footing with some of the best in the world, and a lot of the program's facets can be traced back to the exchange of ideas between Lou and Tarasov.

Be your own manager; don't try to be the manager who came before you. Lou could have viewed following on the heels of the legendary Herb Brooks and the 1980 Miracle on Ice as head coach of the 1984 Olympic team as a source of pressure. Instead, he saw it as an opportunity. As a competitor, he wasn't pleased with the team's performance in 1984, but he knows the players and coaches still did USA Hockey and the country as a whole proud through their hard work and character. Lou never tried to be Brooks. He simply tried to be Lou Vairo. New managers will often hear things like, "That's not how we usually do it," from staff in the initial period they're in charge. It's important not to succumb to the pressure to do what your predecessor did, and to stick with the approach you believe is the right course of action, and the one that makes you most comfortable.

Identify good leaders and good characters on your team, who step up in times of adversity. Managers cannot go it alone in times of crisis. They need the support of lower level staff and managers to succeed. But not everyone can thrive under pressure. Lou looked at how players on his teams treated their teammates and performed in all situations, both good and bad. The true leaders, he says, were the ones who continued to display grit and character — and class — when the going got rough.

When faced with a crisis, form a team. When the International Olympic Committee voted to drop wrestling as a sport from the Summer Olympic games in 2020 and 2024, wrestling leaders

123

worldwide joined together to address the crisis. Bruce Baumgartner was part of that team. Bruce has expertise as a wrestler, and as an athletics administrator, but by his own admission he does not have the skills needed to rescue the sport on his own. The story is illustrative of the fact that sometimes the best thing a leader can do in a time of crisis is ask for help. Leaders don't need to know everything; and they need to admit when they don't. When crisis hits, form a team to meet the challenge—include members from different departments and/or backgrounds who have the skills or expertise needed to solve the problem. The Committee to Preserve Wrestling featured current and former wrestlers, coaches, administrators and executives with experience in marketing, finance and management. All of these were important in its successful efforts to have the sport restored to the Summer Olympics.

Keep emotions in check. As Bruce points out, human nature often leads all of us to ask, "Why me?" whenever something bad happens, in life or in business. For managers, it is important to fight this impulse. As Bruce notes, "screaming and hollering" and looking for someone to blame ultimately doesn't solve a problem or address a crisis. "Stay level-headed," as Bruce says. This sets a good example for those in your charge and enables you to keep your head clear and think of actual solutions to the problem at hand.

Be prepared for change by being prepared *to* change. If there is one lesson to learn from wrestling's fall (or at least stumble) from grace, it is that avoiding complacency can help you avoid problems. Organizations can avert some crises simply by being nimble and open to change. Companies with long, successful track records don't achieve that by doing business the same way year in and year out—they change to meet the changing demands of the times. Or better yet, they change to stay *ahead* of these changing demands.

Stay ready. When Mark Gubicza was left out of the postseason starting rotation by Royals manager Dick Howser in 1985, he could have sulked. Instead, he prepared himself to pitch—everyday. The approach paid off. When he was called upon to pitch the pivotal Game 6 in the American League Championship Series that year, he threw a gem and helped his team make it to the World Series, which they eventually won. The story illustrates that plans don't always work out. Be prepared for emergencies and have contingencies in place when things don't quite work out like you had them drawn up.

Stay positive. Gubicza's story about the pitching coach who came out to the mound to criticize the pitcher during poor outings speaks volumes about how the demeanor of a leader can have an effect on the team. If your employees see you angry or flustered in times of crisis, they will take cues from you. Similarly, if they see you more concerned with finding someone to blame for problems, they will be more focused on that, too.

Identify team members who are committed to the cause. Anyone who dedicates their life to a cause—be it a military or social one—has shown a tendency to remain committed, even in the face of adversity. Managers need to be able to identify these same qualities within their teams. Who is committed to helping the company out of a crisis? Who is looking to jump ship and find another job when crisis hits? A company of loyal, committed employees will always succeed.

Have a crisis checklist. Even the best-trained, best-drilled Navy pilots, and football players, need to have mental checklists, reminders of what to do in certain situations. That's why Navy sailors perform drills, and that's why athletes practice. Have procedures and protocols in place for every function within your division or organization, so that if someone needs to step in and take on a new task on short notice, they have the information they need to hit the ground running. Update these procedures as needed, and train and re-train staff until they become rote.

Make everyone on your team feel important. McConkey is being modest when he says he played the least important position— punt returner—on those Super Bowl-winning Giants teams, but his point about making everyone on the team or within the company feel important still rings true. If crisis hits, everyone will need to pull together. In some cases, all employees in the organization, those at the top as well as those at the bottom, will need to make sacrifices. They may need to work extra hours or take pay cuts. Getting this type of loyalty and esprit de corps from staff is as easy as making them feel part of the team every day, in each and every thing you do as their manager. Sounds cliché, but it's true.

Teach the why, not just the how. Great advice from Jackie's husband and coach, Bob Kersee. Often managers have difficulty delegating, particularly in times of crisis, because they believe they are the only ones who can handle the task. But being a good manager means being a good teacher and empowering your team to take on the challenges and perform the necessary tasks to resolve the crisis at hand.

Take a deep breath. As Jackie admits, this is easier said than done. But while it's important to be proactive, it is also important to make the right decisions and take the *right* actions. And more often than not, that takes time. So even when crisis hits, take a time out and give your mind a chance to evaluate the situation.

Make progress at your own pace. More great advice from Jackie's high school track coach. Our competitive nature often drives us to press ahead, to do better than those we see as adversaries, both within the organizations in which we work as well as in the external marketplace. But while competition is healthy, it's also important to remember that no one wins if you take on a challenge you are unprepared for and fail. Take time to learn and advance when you are ready. It may take a bit longer, but you'll likely find that the success you achieve will endure.

Acknowledgments

It has often been said that a reporter is only as good as his or her sources. This is particularly true in a project such as this one, which relies heavily on the wisdom and insights of its subjects. In this regard, I could not have been more fortunate. My thanks to Bruce Baumgartner, Mark Gubicza, Jackie Joyner-Kersee, Nancy Lieberman, Phil McConkey, Mike Richter and Lou Vairo for sharing their time, experience and expertise.

I also owe a debt of gratitude to those who facilitated contact with these sports personalities, namely Gary Abbott at USA Wrestling (Baumgartner), Eric Kay with the Los Angeles Angels of Anaheim (Gubicza), Alyssa Romano with Octagon Sports Management (Lieberman), Healthy Planet Partners (Richter) and Pat Hanlon and Phyllis Haynes with the New York Football Giants (McConkey). Thanks also to Diane Martella, who assisted in transcribing the interviews for this book. Finally, many thanks to my friend and editor at Strawberry Books, Patrick Quinlan, for his ideas and inspiration.

About the Author

Brian P. Dunleavy has been working as a journalist for more than 25 years. He has covered a variety of sports over the course of his career, including college football and basketball, professional football and basketball, baseball, hockey and soccer. He has written about sports for *The Village Voice*, where for seven years he covered the New York Giants, and he is currently a regular contributor to *First Touch*, a soccer magazine. He lives in New York City with his wife and their two dogs.

SB

A Strawberry Book
www.strawberrybooks.com

www.ingramcontent.com/pod-product-compliance
Lightning Source LLC
LaVergne TN
LVHW021507080426
835509LV00018B/2429

9 780988 213838